"*The book has useful trout fishing information, including a section with 110 trout fishing tips. But it's also about life experiences, the importance of friendship and the beauty of nature.*

In 'A Trout's Eye View,' Thurston gives a detailed scientific explanation of how trout see, and then applies the knowledge to a fishing strategy."

— Bob Riepenhoff, *Outdoors Editor*
Milwaukee Journal Sentinel

D1606150

"*Trout fishing, more than some other outdoors quests, is an ecological and philosophical escapade. Trout fishers will understand and relate to Jay Thurston's message. Folks who have never held a pole, let alone a wild brook trout, will wish they had waded in the trout waters Jay has written about. Many will follow in his tire and boot tracks after reading the words he scribed for this book; if not physically, at least cerebrally. If you can't fish Thurston's haunts, at least read and dream about them.*"

— Jerry Davis, *Wisconsin Outdoor Journal,*
LaCrosse Tribune

"*This book is more than just a good title. Contained between the covers is a treasure trove of prose to delight even the armchair anglers among us. These 60 essays contain in them the spawn of much fishing knowledge. No fishing tall tales here, quite simply because Thurston does not need them.*"

— Eric Hjerstedt Sharp, *The County Journal*

"I have never met Jay Thurston but I can tell from reading this book that our angling lives have many, many parallels. We both love everything about trout streams, their inhabitants and their surroundings. We have both decided that wading stealthily upstream is the best approach for catching wily trout. And, while we both will wield a fly rod on occasion, casting and retrieving lures, especially weighted spinners, is our favorite method. Jay has done a wonderful job of entertaining us with his stories while at the same time incorporating trout tips to make us more successful at catching trout. In case you missed some tips as you read his stories, Jay has emphasized all 110 trout tips at the end of the book. Enjoy the book and go trout fishing soon"

— Jim Bedford, author, *Steelhead Savvy* & *Flyfisher's Guide to Michigan*

Following in the Footsteps of Ernest Hemingway

9-19-16

Please read + enjoy!

Jay Ford Thurston

savage PRESS

Box 115, Superior, WI 54880 (715) 394-9513

First Edition, Third Printing

© Copyright 2005 Jay F. Thurston

ISBN 1-886028-73-7

Library of Congress Catalog Card Number: 2005902497

Published by:

    Savage Press
    P.O. Box 115
    Superior, WI 54880

218-391-3070

Email: mail@savpress.com

Visit us at: www.savpress.com

Printed in the USA

Following in the Footsteps of Ernest Hemingway

And Fifty-Nine Additional Trout Fishing Stories

JAY FORD THURSTON

DEDICATION

This book and the following poem are dedicated to trout fishing friend Pat Hogan; and to all who, when wading a trout stream, enter another world.

Where He Wanted To Go

Slowly he waded upstream
And cast the quiet pool.
Then to the murmuring riffle
And up to the gentle bend.
In the early morning fog
He disappeared from view.
He was gone, he was gone,
Where he wanted to go.

INTRODUCTION

The setting for most of my trout stories is northern Wisconsin, the Lake Superior region. Some, however, took place in the driftless region of west central and southwestern Wisconsin. And one, the lead story, took place in the Upper Peninsula of Michigan.

All the stories are true. Even the length of the trout caught and released was not stretched. When I started this project a few years ago a good friend who was working on his third book told me, "Jay, remember you are writing history. Your stories will live long after you—They must be accurate."

All of the stories originally appeared in *The Daily Press* (Ashland, Wisconsin) June 3, 2000 to September 18, 2004; most also appeared in *The Bayfield (Wisconsin) County Journal.*

Originally I had planned on writing trout stories only for trout anglers. However, I found that many women, some of whom had never fished trout, enjoyed reading my stories. The stories reminded them of their dads—of their late husbands. So then my wife, my dog, a recipe, and the grocery store weaved their way into my trout stories.

Every second Wednesday I was a scheduled guest at a nursing home in Ashland. At each visit, I read a trout story that had recently appeared in *The Daily Press* to a group of residents. Soon my goal changed from trying to entertain them through reading one of my trout stories to getting them to smile, to laugh, and to communicate. So I added some unique experiences (other than catching trout), and occasionally, when it fit, some humor entered my stories. I encouraged them to interrupt me as I read. While reading *Summer Fishing: Fish Early, Reminisce Late,* a little lady put her hand on my arm and said, "My husband went fishing trout early in the morning. When a friend didn't arrive before the sun came up he left without him. My husband told his friend, when you fish trout you have to go early because all the trout are asleep by noon."

"I really like that—all the trout are asleep by noon." I smiled at her; she smiled back. "Your husband was right," I continued, "it's important to get out early in the morning because all the trout are asleep by noon!"

An elderly gentleman with a young mind looked up from his wheelchair and stopped me in the middle of a story. "Jay, you love trout fishing. You know, there are some women here at this nursing home who think they are too old to fall in love." Two women who were dozing off jerked to attention.

I thought, "Do I want to go there?" Then I responded, "Yes, I love trout fishing. I love my wife, my dog, and I love that first flower that comes up through the last snow each spring. We are capable of loving lots of things, including each other. What are some things you love?" We had a good lively discussion—I never finished the story.

You'll find a trout tip in each story, but in some it's more apparent than others. And you'll probably find some good words to live by—thoughts that will enrich or even change your life.

Most of the stories in this book have been shared with the residents at an Ashland nursing home. Please share some of the stories again. When you find a story you especially like, share it with a child, grandchild, or an adult shut-in.

Thank you for buying my book. Read, share, and enjoy!

— Jay Thurston

Contents

Stories with Trout Tips and a Chronology Spring to Fall

Following in the Footsteps of Ernest Hemingway

Ernest Hemingway on the Big Two Hearted River: At the second cast there was a swirl like the explosion of a depth bomb, the line went taut and the rainbow shot two feet out of the water... He measured twenty-six inches and weighed nine pounds and seven ounces.
> – Hemingway, *Toronto Star Weekly*, August 28, 1920

In September 1919, Ernest Hemingway and two friends got off the train at Seney, in the Upper Peninsula of Michigan. Hemingway described in a letter camping out near the Fox River and the three of them catching over two hundred wild brook trout—some up to two-and-a-half pounds.

May 18, 2002, eighty-three years after Hemingway, I was camping north of Seney and fishing the Fox River with Bill Swenson, a retired biology professor from UW-Superior. The river looked high and fast and was difficult to wade. We exchanged corner pools using spinners where Hemingway had used grasshoppers. Hemingway caught trout for supper. The only action we had was from pesky mosquitoes. Instead of trout, we fried hamburgers.

Bill and I discussed our fishing strategy for the next day and decided to pack up and drive sixty miles to the Two Hearted River. Maybe we would find steelhead in the Two Hearted, reported to be Hemingway's favorite Michigan trout stream.

We stopped at a Department of Natural Resources office in Newberry. I inquired, "Are the steelhead still in the Two Hearted?" The polite lady receptionist immediately got someone on the phone. She reported, "He says there are lots of steelhead from the Reed Green Bridge to the mouth. You should have a heyday."

We set up at the campground east of the bridge on the north side of the river. Upstream from the campground, with high expectations of a heyday, we cast spinners into the tea-stained water of a river larger than the Brule. Every twenty minutes we changed lures—no success. After two hours we concluded the steelhead were not in that section of the Two Hearted. Maybe we would find them further downstream, near the mouth.

While at the picnic table eating hot dogs with mustard and onion, we looked over the article written by a twenty-one-year-old Hemingway: "The Best Rainbow Trout Fishing." It was first published in the *Toronto Star Weekly*, August 28, 1920. He described the area on the Two Hearted where he landed a nine-pound, twenty-six-inch steelhead. "A high pine-covered bluff that rises steep up out of the shadows. A short sand slope down to the river and a quick elbow turn with a little flood wood jammed in the bend and then a pool. A pool where the moselle-colored water sweeps into a dark swirl and expanse that is blue-brown with depth and fifty feet across."

I put the Ranger in four-wheel drive and headed toward the mouth down a sand-filled road. We stopped three times to look at the river before finding a sandbank and pool with flood wood jammed in the bend.

We walked among giant white pines along the sandbank of the river. It was steep, about sixty feet above the water. At the end of the turn was a tree leaning down to touch the water. Against it, flood wood was jammed. This was "Hemingway water." Below the pool where the swift river widened we used wading poles for support and cautiously waded across the river. We cast into the deep side, fishing with deliberation. The only sound in that wild country was the trickle of water over logs and the humming of mosquitoes. Deep shadows gathered as the sun floated into the tall pines. A hatch was on, and nothing was rising. As we cautiously waded back across the river we knew we were at least a day late to have a "heyday" trout fishing. The steelhead had left for the cold waters of Lake Superior.

Back at camp, Bill stated, "The grass isn't greener on the other side, is it?"

"Not at all. If we were home we could at least catch brown trout."

At the first hint of daylight we packed up and drove west on a dusty road. We stopped to look at the water from a bridge on the Sucker River. A large fish tailed its way upstream from beneath the bridge. We exclaimed in unison, "That's a big steelhead!"

Less than a mile above the bridge at the tail of the pool, and above a log, I waded in and cast under a hanging tree. I allowed my spinner to settle deep, and then started the slow retrieve. Three cranks of the reel and he hit. I couldn't keep him in the pool. The drag hummed as he raced under the log. Bill watched the battle. I jammed my rod tip down into the water to keep from getting hung up on the log. The line held, and I turned the stouthearted fish into the current. Slowly I gained line and brought him back into the pool. Stubbornly he came to the net. Bill snapped some pictures and then measured my fish. "Exactly twenty-six inches!" he exclaimed.

"The same size as Hemingway's," I countered, as we watched it disappear into wine-stained water. Hemingway, we think, ate his steelhead—maybe with moselle wine? A different time, a different rationale.

On the way to Grand Marais for pie and coffee I said, "When you are away from home you have to search for green grass."

"And like most good things in life," Bill philosophized, "it's not where you expect it."

When Bill Swenson, from Superior, and the author followed in Ernest Hemingway's footsteps they found big steelhead but not in Hemingway's favorite trout stream.

Trout Fishing Can Teach Life Lessons

*The stream is an endless feature of the landscape it forms. It is the
stream that is permanent, and I am only a visitor.*

If you ask ten fishermen why they fish trout, you will probably
get ten different answers. However, all will agree fishing trout
makes them feel good.

Although there are dozens of reasons to pursue wild trout, I concentrate on two in this chapter. First, through trout fishing we can
confirm our existence. Second, we have an opportunity to learn
from nature.

Confirmation of Our Existence

No need to check for e-mail three times a day. No need to look
in the new phone book to see if we're listed.

In our technological world we have limited the use of our senses.
When wading up the Little Sioux River, or down the Big Brule, we
have an opportunity to experience nature directly through all five
senses. We know we're taking up space on Planet Earth and we
don't have to check our e-mail for confirmation.

We smell the sturdy pine and the damp earth. We see the arching cedar and the jack-in-the-pulpit. We taste the wild strawberry
and the blueberry. We feel the water pushing against our waders,
the wild trout struggling to be free, and the tag alder that knocks
the cap off our head. We hear the burst of a grouse taking flight, the
wind quaking poplar leaves, and water cascading over rocks. Our
senses are giving us sustainable feedback. E-mail, the cell phone,
and digital TV are not a part of nature's vocabulary; and when
you're on a trout stream, they are a distant memory that doesn't
compute.

My son Dan was a high school freshman the first time I brought
him north to fish the Brule. On our way out from the river Dan said,
"Dad, this river is so beautiful it doesn't matter if we catch trout."
I smiled deep within, knowing Dan was much further along than I
at his age.

Learning from Nature

Fifteen years ago, on a warm spring day, I was fishing the Bad Axe River, in Vernon County, south of La Crosse. The Bad Axe is an excellent stream—one I rate in the top ten in Wisconsin. However, on this day it wasn't catching large brown trout that drew my attention.

The sun was warm and it was comfortable fishing in short sleeves. I was alone, above the other anglers at the bridge. The only sound was that of the stream against my waders and my reel retrieving line. Suddenly, I heard a light thud. I turned to see a clod of dirt fall down the steep bank and loosen two smaller clods. They rolled into the river to be carried away by the current as they slowly disintegrated.

The stream, I thought, continues to work, although without schedule; it wears at the land. And often, too slowly to observe, it changes the surface of the landscape surrounding it. The stream is an endless feature of the landscape it forms. It is the stream that is permanent, and I am only a visitor.

In Search of the Perfect Recipe
on Stove and Stream

*The joy isn't just in catching fish; it's in experimenting and
trying something new. It's in the search of knowledge.*

Sometimes I feel like I'm a guinea pig when my wife, Diana,
wants to try a new recipe. But that's OK. She is a good cook and
I'm one who likes to experiment. Besides that, it usually works out.
Last week, however, that new pancake recipe wasn't so good. It
turned out too soggy. I thought the recipe called for too much butter.

A lot of the new recipes Diana tries are found in the Midwest
Edition of *American Profile* that comes in the Saturday newspaper.
Recently she handed me a copy of *American Profile* with the page
opened to a recipe titled "Pork & Bean Bread." Diana said, "It does-
n't sound very good, but read what it says and see what you think."
Katie, our black Labrador, who was asleep on the couch, woke up.
Whenever Diana talks to me, Katie usually wakes up.

I read aloud the comment from the author. "'Ten years ago a
friend gave me a loaf of this bread with the recipe. She told me not
to tell anyone that the main ingredient is canned pork and beans.
No one has yet guessed the secret ingredient, but many have
enjoyed this bread.'"

I looked at Diana and Katie. "Let's give it a try." Then my mind
slipped into trout fishing—easy to do any time of the year.
"Sometimes the strangest things really work out well," I said, thinking of the time I had used a spinner blade that had been painted
pink. While Katie went back to sleep, Diana wrote down some
ingredients she needed to buy for the bread recipe.

In a dictionary I found two definitions for *recipe:* (1) A list of
ingredients and set of cooking directions for a dish; and (2) A
course of action recommended for producing some results.

As Diana started assembling her ingredients for making Pork
and Bean Bread I was assembling spinners and paint for a course
of action to get results fishing trout in March and April.

My trout fishing friend from Trempealeau County, Pat Hogan,
came through with an e-mail message which helped define his

course of action. He had ordered the parts (ingredients) to make some large, size-three silver spinners. We had agreed the trout would be deep in big holes during early spring. And it would take a wake-up call to get their attention in cold water. So I purchased some fluorescent chartreuse, pink, and orange paint. The right shade of bright pink was the most difficult to find until I walked by a rack of fingernail polish. There was a small bottle labeled "Heatwave 270, Hot Shade." "Should I?" I thought. "What if the checkout lady gives me the look?" My reach for the bottle stopped in midair. I decided I would just 'fess up and tell her it's for painting trout spinners! My hand grabbed the bottle of hot pink fingernail polish as I immediately headed to the oldest checkout lady I could find.

Back at home, Diana started mixing ingredients for Pork and Bean Bread. Katie was sitting at attention, watching Diana. Secret ingredient? You couldn't fool Katie, not with that nose. I was going through boxes of spinners to select some large silver Mepps and Panther Martin spinners for painting.

The sweet aroma of fresh bread filled the kitchen. After I encouraged Katie to help me beg, Diana relented. Thus, Katie and I gave the Pork and Bean Bread our official taste test. "Really good!" I exclaimed. "It kind of tastes like banana bread." My highly trained dog whined for more. Following the second piece of warm bread I continued, "Remember when you baked zucchini bread and gave Dad a loaf to eat? He told you it was really good banana bread. You knew better than to tell him it was made from zucchini. He would have called it squash bread, and that just doesn't sound good, does it?"

So Diana decided to keep the main ingredient a secret. And if people want to think her Pork and Bean Bread is banana bread, that's OK.

Now I'm painting large silver spinners to wake up big brown trout and steelhead this spring. I'll try a number of combinations with my three colors. Maybe I'll find something that works extremely well. But if I don't hit on a hot color, and my spinners turn out to be like that soggy pancake, that's OK. The joy isn't just in catching fish; it's in experimenting and trying something new. It's in the search for knowledge. And I guess as long as Diana is willing to try a new recipe, and I keep trying different color combinations on spinners and flies, we'll continue to find a lot of pleasure in what we do.

18

In the early season trout need a wake up call.
Fish the big pools with bright colored lures.

Early Season Trout Fishing Provides Opportunity

Big trout are easier to find in April than any other month. With the snow gone, no leaves on the trees, no weeds to walk through, and no mosquitoes, you walk further and fish longer. As a result, you get into areas seldom fished where large trout hide.

If you're there at the right time, you will have an opportunity to catch and release your largest trout when fishing during April. Although large trout over twenty inches are scarce, I believe if you find them, you can catch them. And your chances of finding large trout are better in April than any other month.

Why April, you ask? I'll give you four reasons. First, there is often less food available in the stream for trout in April than May through September. Second, the water temperature frequently rises above the magic forty-degree mark on many April days. When water is touching ice or snow, the temperature will remain at or below forty degrees. Trout feed in the spring when the water temperature rises above forty degrees. And feeding slows down considerably when the temperature goes below forty—it's predictable. Remember, the body temperature of trout is the same as the water they swim in. As water temperature increases, the metabolism of trout speeds up and more food is required. Third, big trout are easier to find in April than any other month. With the snow gone, no leaves on the trees, no weeds to walk through, and no mosquitoes, you walk further and fish longer. As a result, you will cover more trout water and get into areas seldom fished where large trout hide. Fourth, big trout want depth and shade. Due to a lack of plant growth along the stream and leaf growth above the stream, there are fewer places trout can hide from predators. So concentrate on areas of the stream that provide April shade: logs in deep holes, an undercut bank by a tree, and north-facing slopes where the sun can't touch the water.

The early season begins the first Saturday in March and closes the last Sunday in April. It's a catch-and-release season only. And you must use artificial lures with barbless hooks. Read the regulations, because most of the streams flowing into Lake Superior are not included in the early season. Specific lower sections of those Lake Superior streams have a special steelhead season that opens March 30. And there is a third trout season called the regular season. It opens the first Saturday in May, at 5:00 a.m.

We in the Northland have more trout fishing opportunities, but with opportunity comes responsibility. For example, if you fish the White River (in Bayfield County) like I do, you need to know what portions are open during each of the three seasons. You can fish above the White River dam, near Highway 112 in Ashland County, to Pike River Road in Bayfield County, from the first Saturday in March to the last Sunday in April. You can fish below the dam to Lake Superior (the section open for steelhead) beginning around the last Saturday in March or first Saturday in April—check your regulations. And you can fish it all beginning with the regular season that opens the first Saturday in May.

Even a genius who reads the *Wisconsin Trout Fishing Regulations and Guide* and depends upon his or her memory will foul up. I start the early season with two copies of the regulations, one in my home and the other in my trout fishing vehicle. Two years ago, my wife gave me a second copy of the *Wisconsin Atlas and Gazetteer* for Christmas. You guessed it: one copy at home and the other in my pickup. Anyone who enjoys Wisconsin outdoors should have the *Gazetteer*—an atlas of detailed maps for the entire state. A lot of the roads mentioned in the regulations are not on the official state highway map, but you'll find them in the *Gazetteer*.

April 4, 1982, I was fishing with my son Dan (a sophomore in high school) on the Bad Axe River system in Vernon County. The limit then was two trout. When I arrived at our meeting place, Dan was standing on the bridge. I asked, "You done fishing already?"

"I caught my two."

"How big?"

"Twenty-two. Both of them."

"Twenty-two inches!" I exclaimed. "You have to be kidding."

Dan showed me two identical heavy browns that measured exactly twenty-two inches.

"Where did you catch them?" I inquired.

"Come on, I'll show you."

In a pool immediately above where Dan caught his pair I cast a number two red-and-white Mepps spinner and landed a twenty-four-inch brown. It was in a deep pool hiding under the roots of a cottonwood tree. In the next hole facing north, a twenty-inch brown smashed my spinner. And it all happened before Dan finished his lunch.

There are a number of streams I want to fish on my early April spring trip to Vernon and Richland Counties. My friend Pat Hogan, who fished with me last year on the Sioux River, will be checking water temperature and stream clarity. I'm anxious, but I'll wait for the phone call from Pat. You'll get a full report.

Asking Permission Can Lead to Big Trout

> When I asked permission last fall to fish here, the wife said it
> was OK, but I'm going to see if her husband is home today. I
> want to be sure he also approves. This is a good stretch of
> water and no one has been fishing it.
> — Len Harris, Richland Center, Wisconsin

The new no-trespass law that took affect September 1, 2001
means trout anglers fishing on private property must wade in the
water. It's referred to as the "keep your feet wet law."

The former law, passed in 1999, was called the "high water
mark law." Trout anglers, duck hunters, and boaters could walk the
banks of rivers without fear of prosecution. However, the high
water mark could extend inland to include the flood plain. This
resulted in abuse by some who camped on private land and walked
through farm fields. Thus, a new law was signed that is probably
too restrictive and also somewhat ambiguous.

Now if you don't have permission when fishing a stream on private land, you must keep at least the minimum of one toe wet.
However, you can get out of the stream to walk around an obstacle.
What is an obstacle? It might be a fallen tree or a deep hole you
can't wade through. However, if you were wearing chest-high
waders, you could have waded through that hole. Could you be
arrested for wearing hip boots?

In early April I was fishing with my friend Pat Hogan in southwestern Wisconsin. Pat had called and said we could hook up with
Len Harris, a trout angler from Gays Mills, known for catching large
trout. "Make the arrangements," I told Pat, "and I'll be there."

With Len showing us the way, we had two days of excellent
trout fishing. And all our stream access was from private land. Len
took us to Crawford and Richland County streams where he had
permission to fish.

Pat and I followed Len to a farm in Richland County. Len
explained, "When I asked permission last fall to fish here, the wife
said it was OK, but I'm going to see if her husband is home today.
I want to be sure he also approves. This is a great stretch of water

and no one has been fishing it." The husband came out of the barn and Len walked over to introduce himself and us. Len was patient, friendly, and courteous. The farmer was convinced we would respect his property. And we received permission not only to fish the stream but also to drive through the pasture to the stream.

By 4:00 p.m. the water temperature was up to forty-four degrees and the big trout started to hit. I cast my number three See Best Mepps spinner next to a log and had a solid strike. My eight-pound test Berkley Fire Line held, and I was able to turn the big brown away from the log and into the current. He stayed deep and pulled hard, bending my seven-foot rod. It was early season catch-and-release fishing with barbless hooks and artificial lures only. I kept reminding myself to keep the rod bent and not allow slack line. Len came with his long-handled net and reached the big brown after the second try. The measurement was made from the marks painted on my spinning rod, and Pat took a quick picture. I eased the heavy twenty-two-inch male into the water and, with a swish of the tail, he disappeared.

Although this was the first, it was not the only trout over twenty inches long that we would catch and release. In one hour that afternoon, we landed another large brown over twenty inches long, and lost two that could have gone thirty.

Most of our casting was from the bank three feet above the water. When playing a twenty-inch brown, I slid down the bank and scrambled to stop my slide at the water's edge. The water was deep; I could have gone over my waders. I called Pat to come and net my fish. He too almost slid into the deep hole. After releasing the solid twenty-inch female, we discussed how a slippery bank was an obstacle. And how the word obstacle was going to cause lots of problems in the interpretation of the new no-trespass law. Len Harris thought anglers should have access to public water within one rod on either side of the stream, and then the word obstacle would not be necessary.

What it all comes down to is respect for property. Which means you must, like Len Harris, take the time to get permission.

Sunday, April 7 we were fishing for a large trout on a stream near Gays Mills. Len explained that the landowners had a permanent residence in Chicago. "Last summer," he said, "I walked down this road up to the farmhouse. I saw some movement in a bathtub in the yard. I stopped and looked down at the ground while I talked to the husband and wife in the bathtub. It was sure embarrassing, but I got permission. The bathtub is no longer in the yard."

Yes, you must take time to get permission. And although you don't know what you are going to walk into, remember it's important to be patient, friendly, and courteous.

The author with a 22 inch brown trout caught in Richland County during April. He and two fishing friends asked permission to cross private land and fish water seldom fished in the Pine River.

A Good Pair of Waders—
An Advantage Over Hip Boots

*I had to get into the water to keep the fish away from the
tree...Step four put me on my tiptoes with frigid water trickling in
over the top of my hip boots. It's some balancing act to turn a
steelhead which is pulling like a horse when standing on tiptoes in
swift water.*

I vividly recall the last pair of hip boots I wore. It was April 2,
forty-three years ago. Dad and I were fishing the Brule River, in
northwestern Wisconsin. It was slow going through the deep snow
to a small eddy below a rapid. The eddy looked promising as a
holding place for a steelhead. Just as my spinner completed a loop
in the current, the big steelhead smashed my lure. For a few seconds I managed to keep the powerful fish headed into the current.
Then it went airborne, twisting, turning, and trying to rip out the
lure. Spray flew as it side-flopped back into the cold water. Without
hesitation, it turned and headed downstream.

Two things could happen, and neither good. It could continue
downstream and run out my line. Or it could turn toward the bank
and run the line into the tree leaning out below.

I had to get into the water to keep the hard-charging fish away
from the tree, and then try to turn it into the current and regain
control. The first three steps into the Brule were fine, but step four
put me on my tiptoes with frigid water trickling in over the top of
my hip boots. It's some balancing act to turn a steelhead which is
pulling like a horse when standing on tiptoes in swift water. My line
held, I kept my balance, and I had the steelhead working into the
current. I maintained control while backing into shallow water.
Fighting the line and current, the steelhead soon tired, enabling this
happy angler, with cold, wet feet, to land his first twenty-six-inch trout.

On that day forty-three years ago, this angler decided to give up
hip boots for waders.

The first wader advantage: they allow you to keep yourself dry
and comfortable.

The second wader advantage: they enable you to put yourself in
the best position to catch the trout.

All my trout fishing is upstream. I learned at an early age, after reading an article in *Field and Stream*, the importance of fishing upstream. Trout face into the current in order to maintain their position. Waders enable me to get in position behind the trout, where they can't see me, to present my lure. Big trout are usually found undercover at the head of the pool, where they have first choice of the food washing into the pool. With hip boots, I frequently didn't have access to the head of the pool. The water was too deep to enable me to get there by wading.

In Wisconsin, we often fish where the banks are five feet or more above the water level. It's essential to get in the water to keep a low profile. With hip boots, one often has to scramble up a steep bank when the stream narrows and gets too deep to wade. This maneuver will frequently scare any self-respecting trout.

The third wader advantage: you will lose fewer lures.

How often have you hung up your lure with a cast just a few inches off the mark? The water is too deep for your hip boots, and you can't quite reach the lure with the end of your rod to free it from the log. The result: another fly, spinner, or hook lost.

My dad, one of the best fishermen I have fished with, never became comfortable in waders. One reason is that he frequently walked more than half a mile to get into his secret brook trout water. It's more difficult to walk in heavy waders. And, prior to the invention of breathable waders, they were uncomfortably warm when you're out of the water. Another reason Dad didn't like waders is because he never purchased a good quality wader that fit well.

To put yourself in position to catch more trout, and larger trout, you should replace your hip boots with waders. However, for your comfort and enjoyment, it's a good idea to purchase good quality, lightweight, breathable waders.

Meandering Is Good If You Fish Trout

> Then the fisherman has a harmless preoccupied look; he is a
> kind of vagrant that nothing fears. He blends himself with the
> trees and the shadows. All his approaches are gentle and indi-
> rect. He times himself to the meandering, soliloquizing stream;
> its impulse bears him along.
>
> – John Burroughs, *Speckled Trout* (1910)

Ten years ago, the year prior to my retirement as an elementary
school principal, I discussed retirement with Bill Freeman from
Ashland. Bill had been retired for about a year and I wanted some
advice from him—what to expect, the good and the bad. I recall Bill
saying that at first he was kind of meandering around from one
task to another. He mentioned direction was still needed. And it
helped to each day write a list of things to do in order to complete
tasks and stop meandering.

I read somewhere that the average stream meanders at the rate
of ten times its width. So if the stream is eight feet wide, it should
meander every eighty feet to be average. I'm not sure how that
relates to a human being. But since I'm an above-average meander-
er, I probably fritter away more than ten percent of my time each
day. The dictionary has a definition of *meander* for the stream and
the person: the stream, to wind and turn in a course; the person,
to wander aimlessly.

A meandering trout stream will have turns of about 90–350
degrees. A turn of about 350 degrees means the stream practically
turns back upon itself, leaving a narrow peninsula. The more the
stream meanders, the more holes it creates on the outside turn in
which trout can take up residence. And a meandering stream will
create many miles of good fishing within a mile as the crow flies.
Thus, good trout anglers seek out meandering streams.

If you are seeking a mate for life, a husband or wife, you probably don't want to pair up with someone who has a propensity to
meander—to wander about aimlessly. However, to have a friend
who meanders more than the average person will add some enter-
tainment to your life.

One March I was fishing Mill Creek, in Richland County, with my nephew Lee McDaniel. All the snow had melted in southwest Wisconsin, robins had returned, and the sun felt warm on my back—a good afternoon to be wading a trout stream. In the first two hours of fishing, I had landed and released only two ten-inch brook trout. I had about an hour of fishing left before reaching the bridge where Lee would pick me up. Suddenly, the stream started to bend and turn—to meander back and forth. I cast into the center of a large hole, where the current cascading down a ripple slammed into a tree and high bank to make a sharp turn. My spinner sank to the bottom and I started a slow retrieve. Five cranks of the handle and the lure stopped. I set the hook and the battle was on. Back and forth it raced, staying deep in the green-gray water. "If it's a brookie, it is the largest I have ever caught," I thought. You can only use barbless artificial lures in the catch-and-release early season of March and April. "Play it carefully, Thurston," I whispered to myself. When it tired and swirled on the top, I knew it was not a brook trout. Seldom am I disappointed to land a nineteen-inch brown. I watched as, with a flip of its tail, it returned to the deep gray-green sanctuary.

Moving slowly upstream on Mill Creek, in the shadows of trees, while timing my movements to the impulse of the stream, I caught trout. Every ten minutes, the time it took the water to move from one tight meander to another, I released a trout.

John Burroughs, in his 1910 book *Speckled Trout*, wrote, "Then the fisherman has a harmless preoccupied look; he is a kind of vagrant that nothing fears. He blends himself with the trees and the shadows. All his approaches are gentle and indirect. He times himself to the meandering, soliloquizing stream; its impulse bears him along."

Early the next morning, with the thermometer at fifty degrees, I drove downhill from Viroqua (in Vernon County), headed for the heavily fished West Fork of the Kickapoo.

Below Avalanche where the river snakes back and forth, meandering through the fertile valley, I cast my lure. A robin redbreast chirped as it flew low over the river. Wild turkeys, black dots moving slowly, were feeding on an easterly hillside. An eagle, with bright white head and tail, slowly turned, riding a thin air current of the deep blue sky. I was blending in with another trout stream—

feeling its impulse. A meandering man fishing sharp turns and catching trout.

John Burroughs, again from *Speckled Trout:* "It runs through his thoughts not less than through its banks there; he feels the fret and thrust of every bar and boulder. Where it deepens, his purpose deepens; where it is shallow, he is indifferent. He knows how to interpret its every glance and dimple; its beauty haunts him for days." I had fished the West Fork of the Kickapoo often enough to be haunted by its beauty—I had to return.

The angler cautiously wades upstream to cast where the Sioux River meanders to carve out a pool.

Spring Fishing, Turbidity Rules

When I can't see my lure at eighteen inches of water or less, the fish also have a problem seeing the lure. And unless you are fishing with bait that trout can smell, you may as well wind up your line and go home.

Water turbidity is both good and bad. The opposite of turbidity is clarity. And we don't want water that is crystal clear. Water that is too clear is something you will find on most trout streams after all the snow has melted in the swamp and there hasn't been a measurable rainfall for ten days. This is an unlikely condition during spring trout fishing in Wisconsin. And it is practically impossible in northern Wisconsin during April.

So if we fish for steelhead during the April season (which sometimes begins the last Saturday in March) we must contend with a high degree of turbidity. Our streams flowing into Lake Superior have some clay as their subsoil. The more clay in the streambed, and the greater the runoff, the higher the degree of turbidity.

From the hundreds of hours I have logged on trout streams, I know my fishing success begins to decrease as turbidity increases below eighteen inches. I determine turbidity by the depth of water at which I can clearly see my spinner. When I can see my spinner at eighteen to thirty-six inches of water, I generally have my best trout fishing. If I can see the spinner at a depth greater than thirty-six inches, the water is too clear and the fish are easily frightened. They seldom come out from hiding to feed. You have to practically get your lure within six inches of the fish to encourage a strike. When I can't see my lure at eighteen inches of water or less, the fish also have a problem seeing the lure. And unless you are fishing with bait that trout can smell, you may as well wind up your line and go home.

An angler using spawn has a real advantage in turbid streams. When fishing with spawn at the head of a pool, steelhead move upstream to the bait, one after another, to grab the spawn sack. This doesn't happen when using artificial lures. Even if you add scent to the spinner or fly, you have to move the artificial too fast to get a strike from a slow-moving steelhead following the scent trail.

What to do? You can add bright color. Fluorescent yarn, with scent, will work. Also, I discovered last spring the new Mepps spinner called "See Best." Yes, you and the steelhead can see it more clearly in turbid water. Last April I began using See Best lures in size 3. I caught and released more steelhead and large brown trout than any previous spring. Of course, more research is needed—and if I ever need an excuse for trout fishing, more research is a dandy.

I have only been at April steelhead fishing for five years. So I have a lot to learn. You have probably noticed, as I have, that turbidity is much greater in some streams than others. This is due to the amount of runoff entering the stream and the amount of clay subsoil in the streambed. The Flag River (in Bayfield County), for example, is the last to clear up among the streams I fish in April. The Brule tends to clear faster than the others. So I generally begin my steelhead fishing on the Brule. Unless it is an early spring, or I use bait, you are unlikely to find me on the Flag River in April.

My goal is to catch, on an artificial, a steelhead at least thirty inches long. I know they are out there, because I lost two of approximately that size. The largest I caught last April was a heavy female twenty-eight inches long. I caught it at 9:40 a.m., April 25, when fishing the Cranberry River in Bayfield County. The big trout hit in a pool below a rapid where the stream narrowed. After a difficult battle, I managed to get it in the net, only to have it flip out. The next time she came to the net, I turned it so she couldn't escape, and the hook fell out of her jaw. I took a picture and released the steelhead to be caught again. Could it be possible that she will be back in that same hole on the Cranberry? She will be larger, maybe over thirty inches.

If you see me fishing steelhead this spring, stop and say hello. Let me know how you are doing; I still have a lot to learn. So I'll be there, on the Brule, Fish Creek, the Cranberry, or the Sioux. And you'll know what I am doing. It's research, friend, and I am enjoying every minute of the study.

Fly Fishing Beginner
Makes Dramatic Progress

"What I like about trout fishing: the challenge of catching fish
that have evolved to feed selectively. Being in the habitat where
trout live—it's a pristine environment. The sporting quality of
trout—they are an elegant fish compared to the others."
                                    – Jason Neuswanger, Cable, WI

April has usually been a difficult month for me to locate and
catch steelhead. And as a result, I needed an alternative, another
place to fish trout in the northland during April. For someone who
uses artificial lures, spinners, or flies, April is fickle—a difficult
month to have success fishing steelhead.

During April, the streams flowing north into Lake Superior are
often too high and turbid. Rising air temperatures cause the
remaining snow to melt, and it results in red-brown, clay-colored
water. Trout can't see an artificial lure. After ten years of experienc-
ing poor fishing conditions for steelhead, this avid angler needed
an alternative. And I found the alternative at a web site titled
www.troutnut.com.

Jason Neuswanger, from Cable, Wisconsin, had designed his
own trout fishing web site. I logged on and saw a picture he had
posted of a twenty-one-inch heavy brown trout he had caught and
released while fishing the Namekagon River (Bayfield County) in
March. We communicated and decided to meet on the
Namekagon. Jason, a twenty-three-year-old avid fly angler, took me
to his secret place where the previous week he had caught and
released five trout over sixteen inches long (including the twenty-
one-inch brown). We were fishing the early March to April season.
It's a catch-and-release season with artificial barbless hooks only.

After following Jason on the river and talking to him about his
passion for trout fishing, it occurred to me that this young man had
established a new learning curve for fly anglers. Jason gave me two
flies he had tied, exact copies of those he was using, and I took
them to Dick Berge for analysis. Dick is a well-known fisherman
and commercial fly tier from Iron River, Wisconsin. He gave nothing but positive comments when he looked at the quality Jason had

tied into the pink squirrel and stone fly nymph. I told Dick that Jason had started tying flies November 3, 2003, the day he received a fly tying kit for his birthday. So he had scarcely five months of experience on the fly tying vice. And the young man had taken up fly-fishing only last summer. Dick Berge wanted more information on this remarkable upstart. I suggested he go to his website: www.troutnut.com.

On the Namekagon River, I watched Jason cast into great trout holding water. We waded upstream, pushing against water that eventually ends up in the Gulf of Mexico. It's a designated wild river, where you fish without seeing a cabin. And unlike the heavily fished Brule in Douglas County, we had privacy—a large section of river we shared only with wildlife.

Jason Neuswanger is on a year's leave from Cornell University (Ithaca, New York), where he had been studying astronomy for three years. During the past year, he had time to rethink his lifelong goals. Due to his avid interest in fly-fishing, entomology, and underwater photography, he decided to change his major to mathematics and pursue a career in Quantitative Fishery Science when he returns to Cornell University.

This is a self-directed young man who set up his own course of study in entomology—a branch of zoology dealing with the study of insects. Jason used an aquarium net to catch insects near the bank of the river. He identified each insect and pointed out that the Namekagon is rich in trout food. Where a freshwater spring flowed into the river, Jason took pictures of insects with his underwater camera.

"Why pictures of insects?" I inquired.

"The books I was looking at didn't have real clear detail of the insects I wanted to imitate, so I decided to take my own pictures to use when trying to tie exact imitations."

The sun felt warm on my back; I was comfortable while gaining a wealth of information following the upstart. The only thing lacking was trout. We moved slowly to a pool at the tail of an island where, Jason explained, his dad had recently caught his first trout on a fly—an eleven-inch brown. On the third cast, we saw the side of a large brown trout, and Jason set the hook when it took the drifting stone fly. The battle was too brief, lasting but a second or two:

the fish turned, pulled, and snapped off the perfect imitation.

"That was a big fish. What size tippet are you using?"

Jason was looking at his limp line and beyond to the hole where the big trout lived. "He broke off five-pound test. That was a really big fish!"

"That trout was big enough to eat the eleven-inch brown your dad released."

"Yep, I would think so," the young angler responded.

Before we parted, I asked Jason Neuswanger what he likes most about trout fishing.

The studious young man explained, "The challenge of catching fish that have evolved to feed selectively. Being in the habitat where trout live—it's a pristine environment. The sporting quality of trout—they are an elegant fish compared to the others."

Jason, you have said it well. As well as some who have fished trout forty years or more.

In less than one year Jason Neuswanger of Cable learned to fly cast, tie excellent trout flies, and catch large brown trout from the Namekagon River.

Fish Upstream and Improve Your Catch

Think about it: most food washes downstream toward the waiting trout. It seems logical to cast above where you think the fish will be hiding, or feeding, and bring your lure downstream naturally to the waiting trout.

Although most of us have someone in mind we believe is best at catching fish, I have news for you: the best is not a human being. We take a backseat to the kingfisher, the great blue heron, and the otter.

Trout learn as fingerlings, when their brothers and sisters disappear, to dart for cover whenever a kingfisher casts a shadow upon the water. Forty years ago, I read that you should fish with the sun in your face to avoid the shadow problem. Better yet, just fish on a cloudy day.

One September evening ten years ago, I saw a large brown, about twenty-four inches, at the head of a pool. I returned September 30 (last day of the season) and made an excellent upstream approach. When I was in position, I cast my spinner so that it would hit the water about eight feet in front of the big trout. Before the spinner touched down, the trout bolted. It frantically swam by me, headed downstream for cover. What had I done wrong? Then I noticed the sun, just above the horizon, coming in over my left shoulder. My spinner, in the air, had put a moving shadow on the water. The big brown was a kingfisher survivor.

In May, on Pine Creek, I came up behind a great blue heron and literally scared the poop out of the bird as it squawked and took flight. The big bird had been slowly and quietly wading upstream, on the shadow side, just as I was doing.

Five years ago, when fishing the South Fork of the White River, in Bayfield County, I picked up a dead seventeen-inch brown trout. The deep hole just behind the head told the story. It was a recent kill by a great blue heron. The trout was too big to eat, and a spearing heron's catch-and-release doesn't survive.

From my parents' home on the East Fork of the Chippewa River, in Sawyer County, we could watch any activity in our "Musky Hole." We were able to observe, on more than one occasion, otter feeding on suckers. The fun-loving otter knew the proper approach was to come up behind the fish in its blind spot. They would swim upstream, catch a sucker, swim back downstream, exit the water, and eat the catch. An otter would continue until eating its fill, catching all the suckers, or tiring of the sport. Through instinct and teaching at an early age, an otter knows it's best to fish upstream.

A few years ago, I was fishing on Rush Creek, in Crawford County, during the early season in March. Although I was fishing where I had previously had success, on this day, I couldn't find a trout. Then, in the new-fallen snow, I found the evidence. Otter tracks, an otter slide, and blood at the tail of the pool. A better fisher than I had been there.

Pour water into a minnow bucket and you can immediately observe all the minnows turning to face the current. All fish must face into the current in order to maintain their position in the stream and to feed properly. Think about it: most food washes downstream toward the waiting trout. It seems logical to cast above where you think the fish will be hiding, or feeding, and bring your lure downstream naturally to the waiting trout. Trout, especially big trout, are suspicious of a lure that moves unnaturally upstream into the current.

We can learn from the kingfisher, the great blue heron, and the otter. They have been fishing trout long before man fashioned the first pole. Fish upstream, and you too will improve your catch.

Are You Ready For The Trout Season?

Breathable waders make it easier to walk that extra mile and get back to areas seldom fished. I had assumed that since they are thin and light, they wouldn't hold up. Man, was I wrong about that!

The first two or three warm days of late winter, and about the time that I receive my first fishing catalogue, trout fishing is on my mind. There are always some new items needed for fishing. And pre-season is the time to dream a little, make plans, get your tackle ready, and purchase new equipment.

Let's start with your fishing reels. Are they full of good-quality line? Have you cleaned and oiled them? Don't use grease on a fishing reel; also, most oil recommended for fishing reels is too heavy. I use Rem oil. Although it's used for cleaning and lubricating firearms, it's also excellent for fishing reels. Keep your oil with you on the stream and in the boat, and after steady casting for one or two hours, oil all moving parts. When you're done fishing for the day, put the reel in an old sock. It will keep it free of dust and dirt. Put your pole in a cloth bag and then into a tube to protect the rod tip and guides from damage.

If you are a fly angler who sometimes uses spawn for steelhead, or an occasional minnow for a big brown, then you should have two fly reels: one reel containing fly line and one with a line for bait fishing. Before casting your first fly this spring, replace the tippet. Monofilament loses strength with age. Also, when you're fishing, check the knot strength of your line about every twenty minutes. For spin fishing and bait fishing, I use Fire Line, made by Berkley. It has a very thin diameter-per-pound test. Most anglers don't pay attention to line diameter. The larger the diameter, the easier it is for the fish to see the line. Fire Line has enabled me to go to an eight-pound test line that has a smaller diameter than the six-pound test line I was using. Put eight-pound test Fire Line on that extra fly reel and use it when bait fishing. You will add distance to your cast, and the line is very sensitive and resistant to abrasion. Fire Line is more expensive than monofilament, but trout deserve the very best.

If you spend a lot of time wading trout streams like I do, then you need good-quality waders and clothing to go with the waders. A year ago, a year after I bought my first breathable waders, I ordered a suit of black silk underwear. Silk underwear? It sounds kind of feminine; I was hesitant to buy it. But ski jumpers had been wearing it. Now I have two pair, and usually wear silk for that layer under my pants when trout fishing. Considering its weight, it's the warmest and most comfortable underwear I have worn. Sure, it costs a little more than cotton, but your comfort is worth it.

Three years ago, I was fishing with Dick Berge, avid trout angler from Iron River, Wisconsin. Dick was wearing a pair of lightweight breathable waders. I asked him how he liked them. "They are light and durable. If you buy a pair, you probably will never wear another kind of wader." He was right. Breathable waders make it easier to walk that extra mile and get back to areas seldom fished. I had assumed that since they are thin and light, they wouldn't hold up. Man, was I wrong about that! Last year I ran into barbed wire twice and thought both times that I had ripped them beyond repair. They were scarcely scratched, and did not leak a drop. I have probably ruined a dozen pair of waders on barbed wire in the last fifty years. You will appreciate the flexibility of breathable waders whenever you step over a log or walk up that steep bank.

It's important to buy your new waders where they have a good supply so you can try on both bootfoot, and stockingfoot with wading shoes, to get a perfect fit.

Last September when my wife and I went camping and trout fishing, I was unable to talk her into using a new spinning rod. She had to use her "magic pole." But she did wear my lightweight breathable waders. And she was impressed! In my opinion, the waders helped her catch big trout more than her "magic pole." Having her wade in my breathable waders was excellent strategy. Those waders are so good that I need another pair just in case I get a hole in the one pair I own.

The second part of my strategy was to buy her a real nice fry pan for Christmas. It was the most expensive one I could find. Recently, when she was in the store and saw how much that pan cost, she said, "My gosh, I didn't know that pan cost that much money!"

"Like I said, honey, it's a good-quality pan. And you're worth it!"

Now I can purchase that second pair of breathable waders—she thinks I'm worth it.

Opening of Trout Season a Day of Anticipation

The young trout fisherman with long strides, still filled with antici-pation, had overtaken me. We should have known better. Rushing to get ahead of the other guy—you can't catch fish with your line out of the water.

The May fishing opener is more often a day of anticipation than a day of reward. Seldom do we have really good fishing on the first Saturday in May. But that doesn't diminish the desire to get an early start. We know all the trout are there, and we think they are hungry, anxious trout. All we have to do is beat the other guy to the best holes on the stream. It reminds me of the November deer opener. You have parked the pickup beneath a dark sky sprinkled with stars. Anticipation is drawing you like a magnet. But you have to wait a few more minutes to find your way under the first rays of daylight.

Even at my age, after fishing forty May openers, I'm still learning. Opening day 1999, I was on Fish Creek, in Bayfield County, at 5:00 a.m. Two pickups were there and others arriving as I headed upstream away from the bridge. I knew of two pools where I had in previous years caught and released steelhead over twenty-six inches. I was moving fast to the first pool. As I came out of the brush, just below a big *S* curve, there was a young fisherman ahead of me. "What is he doing here," I thought, "ahead of me and approaching my first pool?" I had planned on catching a large steelhead in that pool. It just didn't seem fair.

There on Fish Creek, at 6:00 a.m. on the first Saturday in May 1999, I became a young man. I literally sprinted through the brush and around the big bend to the next pool. I had given up one of my favorite pools—I was not about to give up another. The anticipation of opening day wouldn't allow it to happen.

I was making my fourth cast in "my pool" when I caught sight of movement to my right. The young trout fisherman with long strides, still filled with anticipation, had overtaken me. We should have known better. Rushing to get ahead of the other guy—you can't catch fish with your line out of the water. And you don't fish well if you allow someone else to take you out of your normal fishing rhythm.

That first Saturday in May 1999 was like many others. The night was cold, down to freezing, and the water temperature was dropping when I, and thousands of others, opened the season. Trout feed in the spring when the temperature is rising. Therefore, it's obviously best to wait until later in the day to go fishing, after the anglers who were fishing at daylight have left the stream. The trout have had an opportunity to settle down, the temperature is rising, and the fishing is good. But who can really think that through when operating under the fever of anticipation?

My teaching career began in northern Illinois. I spent ten years teaching in Aurora and De Kalb, Illinois, before moving back to Wisconsin.

There were, as far as I knew in the late 1960s, two trout streams in Illinois. In the spring of 1969, I opened the season on a pretty little stream flowing through White Pines State Park. It's located in northwest Illinois, north of Dixon. It was a beautiful place, among the tall pine trees and limestone cliffs, to take the family for a picnic. It was not the place for a fisherman who had learned to fish trout in the Upper Peninsula of Michigan. Every pool had to be shared. It was impossible to wade the stream, or to easily move from one pool to another. Illinois anglers didn't move around. They fished trout like you would fish bluegills.

I explained my lack of success on my first Illinois trout opener to a teaching friend, a resident of Illinois. He was determined to prove to me that Illinois had good trout fishing. The next year, 1970, I was invited to fish the Illinois opener with my friend and his dad. We went to the trout ponds at Coleta, a small town located northwest of Sterling and Rock Falls. Just like my friend said, there was good fishing at Coleta. And I did manage to catch my limit of trout. However, I had to make a few adjustments. The people who were lined up on my left and right, shoulder to shoulder all the way around the pond, frowned upon my casting. And the trout refused to hit a spinner or fly. It was cheese they wanted. "Jay," my friend said, "just roll that Wisconsin cheese into a small ball and put it on your hook, set your cork for three feet, and throw it out." Sure enough, it worked, and I too started catching trout. They were identical trout, eight inches long. And they had a strange taste—not at all like the wild trout I had caught in Michigan and Wisconsin.

I know we have it good here in northern Wisconsin. Only on opening day do we have to share part of a stream. Even then, we can move and fish at our own pace. Or we smile and sneak through the brush to get ahead of the other fellow.

Trout anglers line up shoulder to shoulder to fish the trout ponds of Coleta on opening day in Illinois.

Cloudy Days Are Good for Catching Big Trout

To be successful as an investor, you don't want to follow the crowd. By the time they figure out what is happening, it's too late. The contrary angler doesn't follow the crowd. He or she will wait for the clouds…and then go fishing before the rainbow appears. After the rainbow, it's too late; the pot of gold has been taken.

The best fishing days are seldom the best weather days, when the sun shines bright. On the warm bright sunny days, it's probably best to grill on the deck, go boating without wetting a line, or head for the beach. But fishing? No, don't even go there.

On the general fishing opener, May 1, I stayed home and waited for the clouds. They didn't come in. But I kept looking to the west while passing time playing a game of double solitaire with my wife, Diana. Although my mind was on trout fishing, I was lucky enough to eke out a victory. Since the clouds failed to show, my wife and I went to Saturday evening church services. There I asked Someone from out of this world to send in the clouds.

While eating breakfast Sunday, my eye was again on the western horizon, and the clouds slowly rolled in to block out the penetrating sun. With a last gulp of hot coffee, I was out of there and on the road to Fish Creek in Bayfield County. Hard-fighting steelhead were calling.

Although a day late, I was not a steelhead short. In fact, in three hours of fishing, I caught and released two big high jumpers and one heavy sixteen-inch brown trout. It was a good opener, and I was convinced once again of the importance of the clouds and poor weather when it comes to catching large trout.

Of course, you have to be sort of contrary to follow the poor weather philosophy. But doesn't the contrary investor do best in the stock market? To be successful as an investor, you don't want to follow the crowd. By the time they figure out what is happening, it's usually too late. The contrary angler doesn't follow the crowd. He or she will wait for the clouds, wait for the rain, and then go fishing before the rainbow appears. After the rainbow, it's too late; the pot of gold has been taken.

Fishing under an overcast sky works particularly well for trout. Avoid the bright sun—the trout do. They will hunker down under cover in deep holes. The sun hurts their eyes. So like the good investor who buys low and sells high, you fish the low sky and avoid the high. Invest your time wisely, and the big fish will reward you.

You can catch small trout in just about any kind of weather. But trout survive to grow large by being reclusive and hiding in the shadows. The trout that acts like a Hollywood star and plays in the bright light has a short life.

That high sun is particularly detrimental to good fishing in the spring before the leaves are on the trees. Without clouds and leaves on the trees, there are no sun blockers. In May, in the Lake Superior region of Wisconsin, the trees don't leaf out in full to block the bright sun until the steelhead have started their downstream migration back to the "big pond." So the best time to fish trout in early May is when there's a cloud cover. It's not easy waiting for the clouds and missing the adrenaline rush of opening day; however, I was rewarded, and you will be too if you are patient when it comes to investing your time on the water.

There were a lot of tracks of trout anglers along the bank where I started fishing at the bridge. But as I waded upstream, the tracks diminished, the clouds held, and the fishing improved. The first steelhead was found in bumpy water below a gravel run where the stream cut under a tree holding fast to the bank. The second came from rapids, bumpy water, at the head of a pool. And the brown trout came out from hiding beneath a log to smash my lure.

At noon, I was past the tracks of anglers and wading into wild country, where I knew I could find more steelhead. But the sun felt warm on my back and the deep blue sky was showing through the clouds.

It was break time, and I moved back from the stream to sit on a large aspen log that a big-eyed beaver with sharp teeth had felled. While eating my lunch, I thought about the morning of fishing—it was an excellent opener. My decision to wait for an overcast sky to begin the season had been a good one. I felt like a proud parent who had tried a new discipline technique with an unruly teenager and it had worked to perfection.

As I write this, I'm checking the weather on my computer. It looks like the clouds will be moving in this afternoon. I'm going to sharpen the hooks on the lure I call "Cowboy." I'll take the long walk and hit some pools where I won't see another angler. Under an overcast sky, "Cowboy" will rope a couple big steelhead for me. Send in the clouds!

Releasing Trout, an Investment and a Gift

> Game fish are too valuable to be caught only once. The fish you release is your gift to another angler.
> — Lee Wulff, Angler, Author

When you release a trout, you are making a long-term investment in the future of the resource. And for that, you can be rewarded more than once. In fact, it could become a "ten bagger." Peter Lynch, author of the investment classic *One Up On Wall Street,* wrote about investing wisely in a growth stock that could grow ten times and become (as he called it) a "ten bagger." Obviously you have to be patient with your investment in order for the stock to become a "ten bagger."

The release of a trout is a long-term investment, and it too takes patience. Lee Wulff became the best-known and most influential trout fisherman during his lifetime (1905-1991). He left a legacy as a writer, teacher, practitioner, and conservationist. He said, "Game fish are too valuable to be caught only once." In 1939 he wrote, "The fish you release is your gift to another angler." Decades before most trout anglers were considering release, Lee Wulff had hung his trout basket on the wall to gather dust.

How about that, giving a trout as a gift to another angler? Probably someone you don't even know. A trout angler you will never meet can have the joy of catching that large wild trout you released. And if it is caught and released ten times, it's a "ten bagger." If you are a patient investor in the trout resource, and a giver rather than a taker, it can happen. In fact, it does happen.

Timber Coulee Creek, in Vernon County, Wisconsin, was known to have one of the highest trout populations in the state. A research study done on that stream in the 1980s, under the direction of Dr. Robert Hunt (a Wisconsin cold water fishery biologist who became well known for his research), found the average brown trout was caught and released five times, the average brook trout fifteen times. Think about it the next time that trout is gasping for oxygen in your hand. If it's a brook trout, you can make a long-term investment in giving—it can become a "fifteen bagger."

Pat Hogan from Strum, Wisconsin, called one July. He said, "Jay, you probably don't remember me. I was in one of your trout fishing classes. You said to call if we ever wanted to fish with you. I thought about it for years, and finally got up the nerve to call. Any chance I could fish with you up there in Bayfield County before the summer comes to an end?"

We made arrangements to fish together in early August 2001. He was the tall, slender angler I remembered from the class of 1985, wielding a fly rod with worms. Pat claimed I had taught him how to spin fish, forget about the worms, and catch large trout.

For our first venture, I had Pat follow me through the woods to the Sioux River. In August, I could depend upon the Sioux for excellent fishing. Following the long walk and descent of a steep hill on that hot evening, we cooled down wading upstream in fifty-six-degree water.

After we caught a half dozen small brown trout, Pat decided on a gold-colored Panther Martin spinner. His rationale: the large browns were probably feeding on small browns, and gold matched some of their color.

We were exchanging corner pools between rapids. It was Pat's turn when we came to the pool where I had caught and released a nineteen-inch colorful brown the previous August. Pat made a cast into the deep water at the head of the pool and the big brown hit. It immediately came to the surface and tried to rip out the spinner. We both knew it would go over twenty inches. And it was a heavy, brightly colored trout. Pat didn't horse the fish; he played it carefully, keeping his rod high. It was a big open pool without obstruction and only a matter of time until the trout was in the net.

Immediately we noticed the depth and color of the twenty-three-inch brown trout. The big male had fought hard and was exhausted; seconds were important to insure survival. The hook had come out in the net. I helped Pat untangle the net and hold up the trout for a picture. Although it was the most beautiful brown trout we had seen, there was no question in Pat's mind what he should do. He held it by the tail while slowly working it back and forth to flex the gills. It took three minutes before it was ready to swim upright into the deep pool.

"Do you think this is the nineteen-inch trout you released last year?" Pat asked.

"No doubt about it. There couldn't possibly be two trout that beautiful."

We discussed how big the Sioux River brown would be next year and what kind of lure to use to catch it. We knew it was at least a "two bagger," and maybe more. Someone else might have given us both a gift.

Pat Hogan, of Trempealeau County, caught and released this large brown trout on the Sioux River. Releasing trout is an investment for the future and a gift to another angler.

Some Stress in Your Life and Mud in Your Water Is Good

A little clay silt in the trout stream, like stress in life, is good; you just don't want too much of it. Trout will come out from under cover when the sky is overcast and there is some murkiness in the water.

You probably know by now that I am sort of an optimist. An optimist will try to turn around a bad situation and find something good in it—like stress in your life and mud in your water. And if you fish trout, you can guess where I'm going with mud in your water. It's all about turbidity. Turbidity, the dictionary says, is murkiness in water due to suspended particles. So the thunderstorm washes small particles into the trout stream and it causes murkiness in what had been clear water. Another dictionary definition of *turbidity* is "muddled in thought or feeling." And in life, that implies stress.

Maybe you're wondering why an avid trout angler would write about stress. Doesn't the angler fish trout to relax and remove stress? A confession: I wanted to get your attention. Even if you're not a trout angler, I believe you should still read my essays.

A retired man I recently met said, "At my age, I don't want any more stress, so I do everything I can to avoid it." He sure got me thinking. How can you avoid stress unless you completely shut down? I felt sorry for the guy. If you want to stay active and involved, you'll encounter stress. Without the low points of life, brought about by turbidity (stress), how can we really know and appreciate the clarity, the high points, and the real joy of life?

We are compensated in a number of ways for the stress we handle. As an elementary school principal, I soon learned that handling problems, although stressful, was a large part of my job. Therefore, I wanted the problems to come to me so that I had an opportunity to solve them. I didn't want them to go directly to the superintendent. I expected problems (stress); it was part of the job, and solving them made me feel good. Solving problems is a part of learning and maturing that makes everyone feel good.

We have had a lot of rain this spring, so many of our trout

streams have been high and turbid. Late in May, I planned to fish Pine Creek, in Bayfield County. However, in the event it was flowing with too much silt (turbidity), I had a secondary plan. And before I left the kitchen with a cup of coffee, I told my wife about plans A and B. (When you fish alone, always inform someone where you are going and when you expect to return.)

When I looked down at Pine Creek flowing under the bridge, I knew trout could not see my lure in eighteen inches of water, so I was out of there. Plan B was to fish the White River, in the Township of Delta, between Pike River Road and Delta-Drummond Road. The upper White flows over rock and gravel instead of clay, so it was flowing clear. And since it was a misty morning, overcast with a few sprinkles of rain coming down, I had excellent fishing. In two hours, I caught and released seven trout from nine to thirteen inches.

A little clay silt in the trout stream, like stress in life, is good; you just don't want too much of it. Trout will come out from under cover when the sky is overcast and there is some murkiness in the water. The clay silt, turbidity in the water, provides cover for trout from predators. So trout come out from hiding and cruise the pool, looking for food. But too much clay silt makes it difficult for fish to see your lure. Eighteen inches of turbidity, I have learned, is just right.

In early June, I was back on Pine Creek. It was a misty morning and perfect turbidity—eighteen inches. I fished upstream through rapids to cast my spinner in corner pools. I was the only angler, the fish were willing, and the steam was mine. I caught and released five trout. And the last trout caught was bragging size—a twenty-five-inch steelhead. The steelhead was unexpected—I thought they had all spawned and returned to Lake Superior. Not expecting a big fish, I hadn't brought a landing net. It was a heavy, dark-colored steelhead, with bright red down the middle from head to tail. It pulled like a horse, taking line out of the pool and downstream under a log. My spinning rod bent almost double as I slowly coaxed it out from under the log and back upstream to the deep pool. But how could I land it? I tried to reach around the gills—too broad and deep. I could hold it by the slippery tail, but couldn't lift it that way. So I knelt down to cradle it in the other arm and it cooperated. I measured the heavy steelhead, took a picture while it held still, and contentedly watched it swim slowly back into the pool.

You can't stop the rain and you can't stop the problems, so turbidity in life and in the water is a given—let's make the most of it.

DEALING WITH STRESS - You can't stop the rain, and you can't stop the problems so turbidity in life and in the water is a given - let's make the most of it.

Clothes to Make the Angler Comfortable

Trout fishing is not a fashion show. You are going to be climbing over logs, stepping around boulders, and walking up and down steep banks... Trout don't care what you wear. It's not style or color but movement that scares trout.

When it comes to clothing and trout fishing, the key is comfort. Will it keep you warm? Will it provide flexibility? Will it keep you dry? You should answer a solid yes to all of the above.

Many people who fish trout also ice-fish and hunt deer. They have learned from experience the necessity of keeping warm and maintaining flexibility. In order to be flexible, we have learned to purchase a coat and pair of pants one size larger than we normally wear. Then we can put layers underneath and still have the flexibility we need to work a lure or smoothly raise a rifle to our shoulder.

How well I remember watching an episode of *Seinfeld* on TV. Kramer bought a pair of skin-tight jeans. He couldn't flex at the knees or hips, and had to walk stiff-legged. I have no idea how he got the jeans on or how he would get them off.

Trout fishing is not a fashion show. You are going to be climbing over logs, stepping around boulders, and walking up and down steep banks. You need flexibility in those jeans. Trout don't care what you wear. It's not style or color but movement that scares trout.

Let's start with the first layer. You will stay warm and maintain flexibility if you wear, next to the skin, a suit of polypropylene or silk. For early- and late-season fishing, I usually wear medium weight. Lightweight polypropylene or silk is perfect for me during most of June, July, and August. In spring, when the air and water temperature are both below fifty degrees, I wear three layers from the waist down. The second layer is wool. I'm comfortable in medium-weight wool pants. Although some prefer hip boots, the third layer for me is a pair of chest waders.

From the waist up, during spring and fall fishing, it's polypropylene. The second layer will be wool or fleece. And sometimes, when it is cold, my second layer is wool, third fleece, and fourth a thin nylon jacket. On numerous occasions that nylon jacket has kept me warm so I could continue to fish during a light rain. However, if you know you are likely to be fishing during cold rain or heavy rain, your outer layer should be a Gore-Tex rain jacket.

Why, you ask, does an old fisherman like me wear polypropylene and wool? As a canoe racer, I discovered polypropylene. It keeps the heat in, is about as flexible as skin, and allows the moisture to escape. Wool? Well, old deer hunters will tell you they have tried all the "miracle" fibers man has made, and none compare to wool—the natural.

What should you wear for socks? If your waders fit tight, you may only have room for one pair of socks. Then I prefer a combination of polypropylene and wool. If you have room for two pair, the first should be polypropylene and the second wool. I like long over-the-calf socks, but they are hard to find. If your socks don't go high over the calf, they will slowly work their way down to your ankles. I have one pair of long wool socks that go over my knee and stay there. I can't find another pair of those wool socks. My wife has been instructed to wash them on gentle cycle.

Serious anglers always wear a cap for protection from the sun and insects. I prefer a wide-brim hat to keep the glare of the sun off my glasses. Yes, I always wear polarized sunglasses that allow me to see logs underwater. Polarized sunglasses help to keep you from getting hung up. When you see the log, you can cast so the current will carry your lure under it. There, a big trout may be hiding.

Does color matter? You bet it does. Mosquitoes are attracted by dark colors, particularly dark blue. So that eliminates all the dark colors. Trout are easily frightened by predators, the wading great blue heron and the dive-attack kingfisher. Therefore, I never wear black, gray, light blue, or white. Over forty years ago, I started wearing a red shirt. I discovered trout were not scared by red—a bright color. It was movement that frightened trout. Trout over twenty inches have followed to my rod tip before seeing me standing there in my red shirt.

Some of the largest trout I have caught were taken during adverse weather conditions. The largest trout I have had on, and lost, hit when I was fishing the North Fork of the Bad Axe River, in southwest Wisconsin. It was a cool and wet spring morning when

I cast my spinner to the head of the pool. I had been told a big brown, about thirty inches long and estimated at twelve pounds, was swimming in that area of the stream. I had made three turns on the reel handle when my spinner stopped. Then it started to move, slowly at first. As I applied pressure, the big trout tore down to one end of the long pool. It stayed deep, and I was trying to apply pressure to get a look at it when it stopped and violently shook, trying to rip out the lure. My six-pound test line separated, and the largest trout I have had on swam free. Sure, I was disappointed, but I was left with the memory, and I have thought about that trout and that day a lot.

I was comfortable wearing a rainproof jacket over wool that day in 1976. If you see me now, years later, I won't look like I'm going to a fashion show, but I'll be comfortable when I am after a large trout on a cold rainy morning.

Going Trout Fishing—Make a List of Necessary Items

Every week my wife makes out a grocery list. She couldn't figure out why I tried for so many years to get along without a trout fishing list. Maybe it's pride—but that too will pass.

Even when I was in high school, when trout fishing was simpler, I went fishing one day and forgot my fly rod. On another occasion I forgot the bait. It happens to all of us; sooner or later, we're going to forget something essential when we go trout fishing.

Just last summer I went fishing with a friend and forgot my spinning reel. Fortunately, he had an extra reel for me to use, and the trip was not a bust. Once I went fishing and left behind my vest that contained all my lures. Since I was fishing early morning, I had to wait until a store opened in a nearby town to purchase a spinner. I bought two spinners and left one in the glove compartment. It's still there, just in case.

I have broken the bail spring in my spinning reel when on a weekend venture. Now I bring along two spinning reels. And I prefer spinning reels with a no-fail-bail. I have torn waders beyond repair, often on barbed wire hidden deep in the woods. Now I bring along two pair of waders.

The mind has good recall of seven things. I guess that is why our phone number has seven numerals. For years, I had a mental list of seven things I needed to take trout fishing: Rod, Reel, Vest, Waders, Hat, Sunglasses, and Creel. Inside my vest were all my lures (plus other needed stuff). So before I drove out of the driveway, I always counted to be sure I had all seven necessary items. The Plan of Seven worked well for a couple decades.

As I have always had a propensity for forgetting over-the-calf socks for my waders, I put an extra pair behind the seat. They are still there.

By 1980 I was starting to release trout. After a few years of putting only spent pop and beer cans in my trout creel, I decided to put a plastic bag in my vest for the cans, and leave the creel at home. Since I was releasing trout, I had to take along a tool with long-nose pliers to help with hook removal. And I decided to take along a camera to capture those large fish on film. By 1990 I was fishing more wild country streams in northern Wisconsin, so I added a necessity, a compass, to my list. The list grew beyond my easy recall when I added a raincoat, net, lunch, wristwatch, pen, and 3 x 5 card.

It sounds like I have missed a few things, right? They are in my vest: insect repellent (two kinds); plastic bag (for those pop and beer cans); box of spinners; box of flies; plastic rain poncho (in case I forget the rain coat); small first aid kit; thermometer (to take the water temperature); Bic lighter (in case I get lost and have to spend the night); and toilet paper.

The pickup I drive belongs to my dog, Katie. So of course she always wants to go along. That is why I need the lunch. Katie waits patiently in the pickup while I fish. She prefers a tailgate party when I return.

My advice: if you can't keep it down to seven or fewer items, you will need a list. And once you start the list, it will grow. Have the list in your fishing vehicle where you won't forget it.

Every week my wife makes out a grocery list. So she couldn't figure out why I tried for so many years to get along without a trout fishing list. Maybe it's pride—but that, too, will pass, like it did for me last summer, when I forgot a reel.

Three weeks ago, I had five shopping stops to make in Ashland. So I made a list. I was about three miles out of town, driving west on Highway 2 and headed for home, when I realized I had only made four stops. Frantically, I searched for the list (which should always be kept in a special place), and found it in the third pocket I reached into. When I realized the stop I had forgotten—the grocery store stop to get three things for my wife—I was four miles out of town. I immediately turned around and went back to the store. Unless she reads this essay, she will never know that I almost forgot.

Even Santa Claus makes a list. Then he checks it twice to find out who is naughty or nice. Making a list is a nice thing to do, just so you don't forget.

Whose Water This Is I Think I Know

The stream gives not only to the landowner, but also to the angler who wades it. The angler who feels the pulse of the stream, wherever he or she originates, gains an intimacy.

One of the advantages we have when we retire is we can choose our time to fish. We don't have to wait for the weekend or a vacation day to hit the water. And having that kind of flexibility, we can choose the best days to fish the busiest streams and lakes. Therefore, we can be on the water when other anglers are not scaring the fish. The fish are then more relaxed and likely to feed. As a result, we often have a good catch.

Generally, unless the weather conditions are excellent for fishing, I don't fish on Saturday, Sunday, or Monday. Why Monday? I like to give the fish a day to settle down and begin to feel secure after being pursued by anglers on the weekend. This strategy is particularly important when you fish the well-known busy lakes and streams. For example, as a retired trout angler, I wouldn't fish the Brule River, White River, Rush River, Prairie River, Timber Coulee Creek, or West Fork of the Kickapoo on a Saturday, Sunday, or Monday.

Tuesday morning, May 11, I was checking out the West Fork of the Kickapoo River, in Vernon County, near Viroqua. There had been a lot of rain in the region over the weekend, about three to four inches. At my first stop, the bridge on State Highway 82, the river looked too high and turbid. It would be difficult for the trout to see my lure. So I drove further upstream, along County Highway S, and found water where trout could see my spinner. I was fishing a section of the river that was designated catch-and-release only with artificial lures. There I cast into plunge pools and beneath lunker structures—all part of the extensive ongoing stream improvement on the West Fork of the Kickapoo. And I caught trout. After fishing for ninety minutes and releasing ten willing trout, from nine to thirteen inches, I put my spinning rod away and headed downstream.

Four men were preparing to fish near Avalanche. I parked beside their vehicles and struck up a conversation as they were assembling fly fishing gear. It always fascinates me why people come from out of state to fish a particular stream. It's something we see now all the time on our well-known Wisconsin trout streams. Three of the gentlemen anglers were ministers who hailed from Dubuque, Iowa. The fourth, Andy Wallace, was from Indiana and the son of Pastor Howard Wallace. This was not an informal gathering that I had entered, but a scheduled tenth annual trout fishing outing for this group, which bore the title "The Honorable Izaak Walton Fly Fishing and Theology Society." I inquired, "Why did you select the West Fork for this year's annual event?"

"We heard about the West Fork from the Orvis Company. Also, a member of our society read about it in *Trout*—the magazine of Trout Unlimited," Pastor Bill Owen explained as he handed me an official copy of their invitation.

The invitation gave information on where they would be staying, reservations, and so on. I noticed a policy statement written in a foreign language. Pastor Owen smiled and happily interpreted for me. "Catch policy: Truly I say to you, thou shall not kill the fish."

It was obvious I was with a dignified group of anglers who enjoyed wading trout streams and fishing together. They told me catching trout was not the main event. Getting together in the scenic hills and valleys of southwestern Wisconsin to enjoy the outdoors was important. There they could wade trout streams that would wash away concerns and leave them relaxed and refreshed.

They were interesting and happy people who made you feel good when you talked to them. I would have liked to spend more time visiting, but I thought they had more important things to do.

As I drove through the picturesque valley, I kept thinking of the anglers I had just met, and about the thousands who come to Wisconsin to fish trout. Trout streams flow through land owned by many individuals, agencies, and trusts. And that ownership must be respected—must be honored. But I also knew the stream gives not only to the landowner, but also to the angler who wades it. The angler who feels the pulse of the stream, wherever he or she originates, gains an intimacy, a feeling for the stream difficult to put into words. Thus I wrote the poem, "Whose Water This Is."

Whose Water This Is

Whose rippling water this is I do not know
Maybe it belongs to all who wade the flow?

They come to ply against the pulsing stream
There to cast and entice trout, it would seem.

The stream to offer only trout would be a mistake
So it's not wild trout the yielding angler will take.

Most will learn what the stream can confide
And in soothing waters, troubles they can hide.

The stream gives a permanence none can reject
And for those who wade rewards they'll collect.

Whose rippling water this is I think I know
It could belong to all who wade the flow.

*Wading trout streams and feeling the current push against his waders
gives the author more than trout.*

Techniques for Fishing with a Friend

For the "Meander Maneuver Technique," use a topographic map to select a section of stream with a lot of meanders. Your partner takes the corner on the left and you cut across to the next corner on the right. You continue fishing this way, alternating meanders.

May 30, 2000, I was fishing Pine Creek in Bayfield County. As I crossed the bridge, near where the Pine flows into Fish Creek, I saw what appeared to be dad and son fishing trout. In a promising hole, Dad quietly instructed his little boy. Son held the magic trout rod and calmly listened to Dad's every word. I smiled and reflected on the first time I fished trout. Dad handed me his fly rod and showed me how to use the current to wash the worm downstream. I landed a bright-colored brook trout, and I was hooked.

Early on May 18, I was compassing through the woods with Ken Belan, from Iron River, Wisconsin, to fish the upper Cranberry, in Bayfield County. Most of the property along the Cranberry River is private, so we had secured permission from the landowner. When we arrived at the river, I told Ken we would use the "Handkerchief Ploy Technique." I stripped leaves off a tag alder branch, tied my white handkerchief near the end, and stuck it in the gravel at the center of the small stream. Ken planned to fish downstream and I upstream. We would meet back at the handkerchief in three hours. Ken was waiting when I arrived to pick up our marker. Together, we had caught and released ten rainbow and brown trout from nine to twelve inches. However, we did not find the steelhead we were expecting—too far upstream, we concluded. The "Handkerchief Ploy" made it convenient for us to fish from a designated spot, then return to that spot and compass back to the pickup. This technique works particularly well when searching for large trout because, by fishing in different directions, twice as much water is covered.

Ken Olson, of Black River Falls, preferred using a technique we call "Hop Scotch." This technique worked to perfection when we fished the Beef River between Osseo and Strum, in Trempealeau County. "Hop Scotch" requires two sets of keys. Before you begin fishing, you decide exactly where your partner starts on the river, where you will begin, and where you will end. Then you drop off your partner. He or she fishes up to where you began (it works best if you begin at a bridge) and, using the second set of keys, drives to where you will end. The beauty of this technique is that you have a section of river to yourself and no one has to walk back to the vehicle.

The late Bob Miller, from Eau Claire, and I fished at exactly the same pace. Therefore, we could use the "Meander Maneuver" to perfection.

For the "Meander Maneuver," use a topographic map to select a section of stream with a lot of meanders. Your partner takes the corner on the left and you cut across to the next corner on the right. You continue fishing this way, alternating meanders. You're close to your friend to admire the large fish and take pictures for memories. You can readily exchange information on lure type, size, and color. With the "Meander Maneuver," your fishing can be more productive and enjoyable.

On June 1, Ken Belan and I decided to fish the Flag River, in Bayfield County. We started at the big hole where the East and West Forks meet. We used the "Two Stream Technique." Ken fished up the East Fork and I waded up the West Fork. Our plan was to meet back at the big hole in three hours. The morning was overcast after a light rain—perfect trout fishing weather. We caught and released thirteen trout from nine to fourteen inches. All of mine, from the West Fork, were brown trout. All Ken's, from the East Fork, were rainbow. Fishing two streams instead of one had allowed us to gather more information. Next May we'll return to the East Fork, and search for that elusive big steelhead.

What Color Lure Js Best

> I have for a long time suspected that there is one color they
> like especially well, and that is yellow. There is no way to prove
> it, but it seems to me that the trout always bite faster when I
> show them a fly with a lot of yellow in the dressing.
>   – H. G. Tapply, Field & Stream

If you have fished one particular lake or stream extensively, you have discovered that some colors work better than others. You might also have concluded that one color works better in August and September than in May.

The debate over what color to use has been going on for centuries. However, we have known for years that most fish see things in living color. Research, in the laboratory and in the stream, has proven that fish with bony skeletons have both rods and cones in their eyes, which enable them to see things in living color, similar to humans. Trout, and all of our freshwater fish that I can think of, have bony skeletons, and can therefore distinguish color. Cartilaginous fish, such as sharks, have only rods and are color-blind.

My son Dan believes trout have an affinity for a color similar to the bottom of the stream. If the bottom is dark brown or black, Dan will use a brown or black lure. If the bottom is sandy, he will use yellow or gold. There is some research that supports Dan's theory, but it was done in a laboratory, under controlled lighting conditions, rather than the natural conditions of a trout stream.

When choosing color, I believe there are three things to consider: the amount of light penetrating the water, the clarity of the water, and the color of the steam bottom. Only experience, or a good guess, can help you when working with so many variables.

If you're not sure what color to use, try yellow. In the July 1973 issue of *Field & Stream*, H. G. Tapply wrote, "I have for a long time suspected that there is one color they like especially well, and that color is yellow. There is no way to prove it, but it seems to me that the trout always bite faster when I show them a fly with a lot of yellow in the dressing." Well, I can't prove it either, but a fly and a spinner with yellow is usually effective. All fish seem to be attracted to yellow when used early and late in the day.

On a Sunday evening in July, my wife and I went fishing for crappies in a lake near our home. I put a minnow on a yellow jig, and we drifted until I caught the first crappie. We anchored, and in the hour before sunset, Diana and I caught fourteen keeper crappies. Yellow has always worked well for me in both lakes and streams.

When I look at the data in my trout fishing journal, I certainly have evidence to suggest what color to use when I fish a particular stream. I usually wait until August or September to fish the Long Branch of the White River. The color combination of black, white, and gold has been effective for me late in the season on the White.

I have discovered the color pink to be particularly effective in May and June on the Cranberry River. It works well for both steelhead and brown trout. My guess is that pink is a color that shows up well in the light clay-colored water of the Cranberry. On June 13, I was using a bright pink-colored lure when fishing the lower third of the Cranberry. I came to a big pool where the river cascades down between rocks to slam into a bank and make a sharp turn. In the pool between the bank and the rocks, I nailed a heavy seventeen-inch brown. At the head of the pool, in the bumpy water, a twenty-three-inch rainbow smashed my pink lure. It was an overcast morning, and pink was the color that enabled me to catch and release seventeen trout in four hours.

When it comes to color, we have only begun to touch the tip of the iceberg. My advice: start with yellow or gold, since fish seem to be attracted to yellow more than any other color. Bright colors work well in the spring and in discolored water. Some colors just work better in some streams than others. Through practice, you will find the color that works best for you in your favorite stream. It is the desire to gain knowledge, discovery through trial and elimination, that helps make trout fishing enjoyable for most of us.

Wading Streams a True Gift

You should face the current, bend slightly at the knees to keep
your balance, and keep your legs separated by more than one
foot, so water can flow between your legs. Then slowly walk
across the stream, taking six- to twelve-inch steps, as you move
your feet slightly forward and to the side.
                                    – Ford Thurston (1905-1993), Winter, WI

Learning to wade a swift stream is not something you want to do on your own. It's best to have someone along who enjoys wading trout streams. Sure, you can read about it, and that will help. But there is no substitute for direct experience on the stream.

I recently read in a national publication about the correct technique to use when wading a swift stream. The author's explanation and picture demonstrated that one should always cross a swift stream walking sideways, slowly putting one foot in front of the next. My dad, Ford Thurston, taught me on the stream. He said, "You should face into the current, bend slightly at the knees to keep good balance, and keep your legs separated by more than one foot, so water can flow between your legs. Then slowly walk across the stream, taking six- to twelve-inch steps, as you move your feet slightly forward and to the side." You should wade a swift stream like an old cowboy walks—an old cowboy who has spent most of his working hours on horseback.

Measure your legs at the calf. Average size is about four inches across the front and six inches across the side. To compensate for this, waders are narrower at the front. Measurement alone will tell you to face into the current when crossing a swift stream. The wider the surface that the water has to push against, the more apt you are to be swept off your feet.

With practice, you can learn to use the secure wading step. Normally, as we step forward we put our weight on our leading foot. For trout fishing, it's best to keep your weight on the following leg until you feel solid footing and can have good balance on the leading foot. This is unnatural, and it requires practice and a slow wading pace. The slow wading pace is needed anyway, in order not to create a wave and spook the fish in front of you.

My nephew Lee McDaniel had done some trout fishing, but had not fished with waders. He was a high school sophomore in Cashton, Wisconsin when he visited in August 1996. Lee was big enough to fit into a pair of my size-ten waders. I took him to Fish Creek for his first experience. Lee, a good fisherman, had no problem casting. I could immediately see it was wading that was going to cause a problem. Although I demonstrated the slow trailing foot balance step, Lee couldn't handle that difficult an assignment. He got a little excited after landing a thirteen-inch brown and was soon off balance on slippery rocks. I helped Lee empty water out of the waders and wring out his socks. We pressed on and, although wet, Lee continued to catch trout.

Obviously, it's best to take the neophyte to a steam where he or she is very likely to catch some nice-sized trout. Then, if the beginner does get wet, it will not be a terrible event, but a good learning experience.

The summer of 1984, my wife Diana and I were traveling the state of Montana. We planned to sightsee, camp, visit relatives, and fish trout. One evening when camping near Wisdom in southwestern Montana, we talked to a camper who was enjoying brook trout for supper. He exclaimed, "I have never had such good brook trout fishing—all native ten- to twelve-inch fish!" All we had to do, he said, was walk about a quarter mile north of the campground and we would hit the creek.

Early the next morning Diana and I were wading up May's Creek. The fishing was everything the generous camper had said. I taught Diana the correct procedure for wading across the swift stream, facing into the current. We caught all the brook trout we wanted for our next meal. However, it was obvious to me that Diana would need more than one lesson before feeling comfortable wading a swift stream.

We had fished about an hour when Diana tried to take a scrappy ten-inch brookie off the hook. It squirmed free and fell into the clear water. "That happens to every trout fisherman," I said. "Don't worry; there's lots of fish here!"

"But I still have it!" she exclaimed. "It's under my boot. I stepped on it!" I could see it in the clear water—head sticking out one side and tail out the other.

"That's impossible!" I exclaimed.

Diana smiled and calmly responded, "I didn't know that."

Diana Thurston, wife of the author, waded many trout streams before learning to wade swift water with confidence.

Give Trout Your Best Presentation

Deliver your lure so it will turn under the cover directly in front of the trout. The food was there, and then it starts to escape. It's too much for the trout to resist.

When I go out to eat, I like to go to a restaurant that gives me a good presentation. The food is attractive. You know it will be good before the first taste. And the service is excellent. Trout have similar eating habits. Usually they like to be waited on, and prefer the food to be presented to them in their place of relaxation.

However, for trout on the move, it is a different story. Trout travel up and down streams far more than most people realize. They aren't particular when they're going places, and it's drive-through time. All you have to do is present the lure in front of them and they immediately smash it. They are on the move and they are hungry. Fast food time is predictable for both people and trout. For people, it frequently happens on weekends and is especially common on three-day holiday weekends. For brown trout, it happens in September when they begin their upstream migration in search of a spawning area. It's common in April for steelhead when they are spawning. For brook trout, it frequently happens in early June when they are on an upstream migration to cooler water.

So there are times when trout fishing is easy. However, we're usually presenting to a finicky eater. Trout don't want to move for food. They want delivery to the door. My guess is a trout fisherman started the first pizza delivery service.

The first essential of a good presentation is to deliver your lure to the home of the trout—to where the trout is hiding. So look for the hiding place. It's usually a log, an undercut bank, or debris caught on a tree or branch leaning down and touching the water. Remember, the big trout hiding under cover will not come out after food. It wants delivery. Deliver the lure so it will turn under the cover directly in front of the trout. Your spinner, or fly, or bait, makes a turn in front of the trout and starts to move away. The food was there at the nose of the trout, and then it starts to move on an escape route.

It's too much for most trout to resist. With practice, you can judge the speed of the current and upstream angle of your cast necessary to make that magic turn, frequently about 25–35 degrees. Most of the large brown trout I have caught over twenty inches long were caught on this kind of presentation. Remember, all fish face into the current. When you are standing to the side of a trout that is under cover, it cannot see you. The cover it is under prevents it from seeing you to the side or rear. It can only see you if you are in front of it, in the direction it is facing.

When you see an area with cover where a large trout might be hiding, don't cast directly on the spot where the trout is. Plan your cast about three feet beyond and above the spot. A cast over the fish would scare it. It's too much like a fish-eating "dive bomber," the kingfisher.

Many anglers fail to recognize the importance of bumpy water as an ideal holding place for a feeding trout. Bumpy water is wavy water, often caused by water rushing over rocks or logs. It's created when the stream narrows and rushes through a narrow gap, causing waves on the surface. Bumpy water provides cover. Predators can't see trout in bumpy water. Essentially, it is cover where trout feel safe.

On the morning of June 6, 2001, I started fishing the Cranberry River (in Bayfield County) where the river flowed parallel to a road. It was obviously an area with easy access and was heavily fished. I noticed bumpy water at the head of the first pool and a large rock just to the right of center. I made a cast about three feet above and beyond the rock. My spinner angled downstream to the rock and then, in the calm water behind the rock, made a turn. The lure stopped, I set the hook, and the battle was on. The twenty-inch rainbow was difficult to control in the fast water. I kept backing downstream to keep the stouthearted fish battling into the current. When I managed to bring it to net, the spinner fell out. The rainbow cooperated and posed for a quick picture. Then I watched it take a couple deep breaths and slowly swim away toward the rock in the bumpy water.

The most important thing to remember about a good presentation is the delivery. Large trout hold under cover. Present your lure so that it makes the magic turn in front of the trout. And don't overlook bumpy water at the head of the pool. Knowing the address is just as important for the angler as it is for the pizza delivery person.

Keeping It Simple

*Listen Jay, do you hear that? Sometimes, I just come down here
to sit on a rock, listen to the stream, and watch the wildlife.*
– John Butler, Grandview, WI

Trout fishing shouldn't be complicated. Sometimes, we fuss
over what fly to use. Or we keep changing lures, and as a result
spend too much time with our line out of the water. We should keep
it simple and fish with the lure in which we have confidence.

Memorial Day weekend my two sons and I met in Winter,
Wisconsin. We were going musky fishing in "Granddad's Lake."
Three generations were there on Blaisdell Lake that Sunday, May
27, 2001. Dad was with us in spirit—we felt it as we fished his
favorite musky water. Dave and I spent too much time looking in
our tackle boxes and switching lures. Dan used his granddad's
favorite lure. That morning, he caught the only musky. Late in the
afternoon, Dan was still using the same bait. A large musky came
up under his top water bait; a giant swirl and the musky was gone.
All the action on that Memorial Day weekend came to the angler
who kept his bait in the water.

Tuesday, June 5, 2001, I saw Lillian Morey mowing her lawn,
and stopped to talk to her about fishing the Iron River. Lil was
raised on a farm north of Iron River, Wisconsin, which bordered the
West Fork of the Iron. Eighty years ago, as a barefoot child, she was
catching large brown trout for the family meal. She was a worm
angler, and found bait under logs and rocks along the river. Lil used
a willow pole she had cut near the river. With a line, hook, and a
nut removed from a piece of her dad's farm machinery for a sinker,
she was the complete angler.

On that crisp June morning, with her lawnmower shut down, Lil
told me stories about fishing trout. She said, "Mother gave me
twenty-five cents to catch six trout for supper. I had my six trout on
a tag alder pole when I was walking up the bank toward home. I
saw a fisherman with all the fancy equipment, hip boots, trout basket, vest, and bamboo fly rod. He hadn't caught a trout, and was so
surprised that a little barefoot girl could fish that well."

How many of us learned to fish trout as Lillian Morey had? We
simplified it, and kept our line in the water that we knew held trout.

Two days later, on June 9, I was fishing with John Butler in his favorite water. We were near the Porcupine Wilderness Area, in Bayfield County, southeast of Grandview. I had walked behind the avid outdoorsman through the balsam. John was on his ATV. After a stroke, heart attack, and four operations, I still saw the sparkle in his sky-blue eyes when we talked trout fishing. I followed as he drove slowly down the hill into a cathedral of yellow birch, hemlock, and sugar maple. He stopped, shut down the ATV, and asked, "Listen, Jay, do you hear that?" I turned my head, listened, and nodded. He continued, "Sometimes, I just come down here to sit on a rock, listen to the stream, and watch the wildlife."

We had been introduced to each other the week before on the phone. This was John's special place where he had gone trout fishing for sixty years. I was a stranger in his paradise. I wanted to savor the moment. Looking at the old growth forest, and listening to the sound of water over rock, I asked, "John, it doesn't get any better than this, does it?" He didn't answer my question. He didn't have to.

We caught and released many five- to seven-inch bright-colored brook trout that overcast morning. John used worms and brought along five size-eight hooks. "Why five hooks?" I asked. He smiled and said, "Some of the small brookies take the hook too deep, and I cut my line to release them so they can live."

Fishing wasn't easy for John. He had his pole in one hand and cane in the other as he made his way upstream on the solid gravel. While I fished a half mile of water and caught one nine-inch trout, John fished fifty yards and caught two, about nine and ten inches. He planned to have them for supper. They came from hiding places where John had been catching trout for decades. Like Lillian Morey, he simplified it and kept his line in the water.

John Butler disappeared in a cloud of dust as he headed up the road to home on his ATV. He had invited me to come back and fish in the cathedral of sturdy old growth trees, where delicate pink lady slippers grow and clear water cascades over gravel. This was John's secret place. He had given me a gift. I smiled and said, "Thanks, John. Yes, I will come back."

Where the Large Brown Trout Swim

In order for a fish to grow large in a short period of time, it must have an abundance of food. Therefore, you need to fish streams that produce lots of food—the hard water streams.

The brown trout, like most of us, is an immigrant. The original shipment of brown trout eggs arrived from Germany in 1883. Fry from that first shipment were planted in Michigan's Baldwin River (a tributary of the Pere Marquette River) in April 1884. Soon shipments followed from England and Scotland. By 1890, the brown trout had taken up residence from New York to Yellowstone Park in approximately two hundred rivers and ponds. English trout anglers often took their prized brown trout with them when they settled in foreign lands. Thus, brown trout appeared in Australia and New Zealand. Today the brown trout is the widest-ranging trout, and can be found throughout the world where suitable water exists. It is believed to be the most intelligent of the trout, due to having survived centuries of fishing pressure in Europe. Thus, in the United States where rainbow, brook, and cutthroat trout are easily caught, brown trout survive.

Brown trout in Wisconsin have attained an age of nine years. In more hospitable climates lacking ice and snow, they can live considerably longer. A brown trout from England lived to the ripe old age of eighteen. The largest stream-caught brown trout in Wisconsin came from the Brule River. Caught August 30, 1940 and weighing in at eighteen pounds, twelve ounces, it was believed to have moved upstream in late summer from Lake Superior. In 1961, a twenty-three-pound brown measuring 34.4 inches was captured when electro-fishing the Little Brule River in Douglas County. Big brown trout are known to move up small streams in August to spawn and/or to find cool water.

A number of brown trout weighing better than ten pounds have been taken in Wisconsin streams. If you wanted to catch a large stream-run brown, where and when would you fish? Remember, when you pursue a trophy fish, you must sacrifice quantity for quality.

In order for a fish to grow large in a short period of time, it must have an abundance of food. Therefore, you need to fish streams that produce lots of food. Hard water streams, those that originate from limestone bedrock, produce considerably more food than freestone streams. Thus, other than fishing the Brule River in late August or September, you will need to fish another region.

The largest trout caught in Wisconsin on hook and line, that was not a lake-run fish, came from the Rush River in Pierce County. The big brown weighed fifteen pounds, one ounce and was caught July 1985. The Rush River is famous for large brown trout. In 1974, it gave up a fish weighing fourteen pounds, eight ounces. Today the Rush is heavily fished, and brown trout like seclusion. So when I fish the Rush River I concentrate on those portions that see fewer anglers. Generally, that means I don't fish those stream areas where I see other anglers, and I frequently walk a ways from the access point before making my first cast.

The Green River, in Grant County, is well known for large brown trout. During the early season of February 1977, a twelve-pound brown trout was caught. It was taken in a snowstorm under the bridge on County Highway X near the small town of Werley. I talked to the owner of the bar-restaurant in Werley (which has since burned down) and he verified the fish. He told me, "I tried to talk the guy out of using a night crawler. I told him it wouldn't be natural food in February. But he insisted on using crawlers. When it started to snow he went under the bridge, and that is where he caught the twelve-pounder."

The Bad Axe River, near Viroqua in Vernon County, has given up some large brown trout. In March 1982, an angler from La Crosse landed a twenty-eight-inch brown that weighed eleven pounds, nine ounces.

Large brown trout exceeding eight pounds are not uncommon in the Pine River of Richland County. Two years ago, when spin fishing in April, I landed a twenty-two-inch brown, and had a big brown hit that I believe would have gone over eight pounds. Last April an angler from Madison had on and lost an exceptionally large fish in the same hole—probably my fish. You know where I will be fishing next April.

What is the best time to catch a big brown trout from Wisconsin waters? The early catch and release season—late March and early April. Brown trout avoid the bright sun, so fish on an overcast day. Concentrate on the streams I mentioned above and other large trout streams in limestone bedrock country of Pierce County (in western Wisconsin), and in Vernon, Richland, Grant, and Crawford Counties of southwestern Wisconsin.

Lee McDaniel, of Cashton, fishes a Vernon County river in April where an 11 pound 9 ounce brown trout was caught.

A Million Nodding Trilliums

It's trout that gets you there where nature is displayed at its best for your enjoyment. But you have to take time to stop and look or it's all the same.

The earth turned and the sun stretched through the leaves and slid down to the river. It was time to quit trout fishing and put our back to the Sioux. Bill Swenson and I had talked about lures, trout we caught, tall trees, deep pools, and lunch. Now we were on the trail as the rapids whispered to a murmur. Then we stopped and bent down to look at a single nodding trillium. "Look, Bill!" I exclaimed. "This one is different: the ends of the petals are a purplish rose instead of pure white." I knew before I stopped that Bill, the retired biology professor from UW-Superior, would be interested in that special flower. We moved on up the slope in reflection. I thought about trilliums and how reverent they appear, always nodding in respect. Because the experience of sharing nature through trout fishing with Bill Swenson had been enjoyable, I couldn't help but think of others I had fished with who would have stopped to look at the magenta-colored trillium. And I thought of the poem I had written, "A Million Nodding Trilliums."

A Million Nodding Trilliums

The floor of the woods again white
Covered by a million nodding trilliums;
From a distance they are all identical.
But each has its purpose, time, and passing;
And so it is with many human beings:
Like the trilliums, they wait discovery.

Like the trilliums, from a distance we all look identical. Look at people on the other side of a football stadium: they all look identical. You have to get close to the person, and the flower, to see the difference. When you see that each flower and each person is unique, you know it is the difference that makes them special. But some people don't stop to notice. Bill and I had stopped, and we knew why. There is a lot more to fishing trout than catching trout. We had caught enough trout in our lifetime to know lasting pleasure comes from the pursuit of trout, rather than the catching. It's the trout that gets you there, where nature is displayed in its best for your enjoyment. But you have to take time to stop and look, or it's all the same—like every white trillium and the people in the stadium.

When I saw that special trillium, Bob Miller came to mind. Like the trillium, Bob was different. He had developed a special reverence for trout fishing. And I would like to think I had a small part in fostering that appreciation. Like the trillium, Bob Miller's time on earth was short. And I'll probably never understand why. For some things, there is no answer.

Bob called four summers ago and it hit me like a thunderbolt. At only age thirty-six they had found cancer in a number of places in his body. But he was being treated, he was fishing trout, and he sounded hopeful. I can suppose Bob thought as I would have: "When the trout season opens I'll start fishing, and I'll feel better." So he put off seeing a doctor and then it was too late.

We wanted to get together to fish a last time. I called, but had to talk to him in the hospital. The next time I spoke to him, he was better; he told me he had fished Lowes Creek, the trout stream flowing by his house, with his dad and a brother. Diana and I left for Eau Claire. If Bob and I couldn't fish, at least we could talk trout.

Bob Miller, his wife Krista, two pre-school daughters, and Kramer, their golden retriever, met us at the door. Bob's hair was gone from the treatment; he looked slim, but he had that broad grin I had often seen on the stream, and the same firm handshake. We sat down in the living room and Bob told me he had waded upstream a last time. His dad and brother had to help him out of the stream. "Jay," he asked, "how can I fish trout if I'm not strong enough to wade the stream?" I was still his trout mentor. It wasn't easy for me; I wanted to cry, but I forced a smile and told Bob how to use a minnow and fish a big hole from the bank.

Two weeks later, as colored leaves floated on trout streams, we were again in Eau Claire, this time at a funeral home. Bob's ashes were in his trout creel and they would be spread in his favorite trout stream, the Bad Axe River. His wife handed me his trout journal. Diana and I read about some of the times we had fished together.

Before I left, his wife gave me a hug, smiled, and said, "Jay, there will be times when you think you're all alone on the trout stream, but you won't be—Bob will be there."

Although nothing fills the void left by a great trout fishing partner, and the tears roll as I write this, Krista was right: Bob has been there.

The Attractor Catches All

*Large trout in an area of the stream with a good forage base feed
less than one hour per day. And they seldom get angry at a lure
unless it invades their secret area... However, they can always be
attracted to a lure.*

I'm taking lures out of my musky tackle box to make room for
some new attractors. Last summer I caught a fifty-two-inch musky
when fishing Lake-of-the-Woods, on a lure I call an attractor. It's a top-
water bait with a unique sound. It took some research, with the help
of my wife, to find the manufacturer of that bait. We were successful,
and this year I have half a dozen of those unique-sounding attractors.
However, on the big musky trip I'm bringing along three new sight
attractors. I have a theory that musky, trout, and people are all attracted by both sight and sound. Of course, more research is needed.
More research—now there's a great intellectual excuse for fishing.

In our summer travels around the country, Diana and I have easily picked out notable tourists. We call them "Tilly and Ted Tourist."
Seven years ago, on a warm summer day, we were preparing to
board a boat at Bayfield to Madeline Island. Simultaneously we
found "Tilly and Ted": a senior couple in shorts with brightly colored
blouse and shirt. Tilly was wearing a silk flowered straw hat. Ted
had on a pair of long dark socks and wing tip shoes. The colorful
couple looked different: they were attractors.

There are three reasons why trout hit a lure. They are hungry, it
makes them mad, or the lure attracts them. Large trout in an area
of the stream with a good forage base feed less than one hour a day.
And they seldom get angry at a lure unless it invades their secret
area—when they are spawning or in a protective mode. However,
they can always be attracted to a lure. And I believe large trout are
attracted by a lure that is different in sight and/or sound. That is precisely why a spinner that looks and acts different is an excellent lure
for large trout. Prior to using spinners for trout, I was casting flies.
Since I had little knowledge of entomology, I tied and used brightly
colored flies—attractors that didn't resemble an insect. In those
early days of trout fishing I landed a lot of fish (not just trout) while
casting a Mickey Finn, a royal coachman, or a silver doctor. And I
still use a Mickey Finn when fishing crappies. Maybe it's time to get

back to my fly-tying vice and create a fly called "Tilly Tourist."

Ten years ago, Diana and I were camping in Montana. We visited relatives, acted like tourists, and fished trout. One mission we had was to find the perfect Montana cowboy. On a rainy morning, we drove from our campsite to a restaurant in Wisdom, Montana. While enjoying breakfast, we turned, along with most of the others in the small-town restaurant, to watch a cowboy. He was tall and slender, with a wide-brimmed hat, cowboy boots, jeans, and a colorful shirt. He had a smile and a swagger as he walked across the hardwood floor. We stopped eating and watched him sit down at the counter. Immediately two attractive young ladies came over to sit on either side of him. We looked at each other and whispered in unison, "We found our Montana cowboy."

Two years ago I discovered a spinner that is a great attractor, and I call it "Cowboy." This year in particular, my cowboy is having a great ride. By June 1, I had caught and released fourteen brown and steelhead trout that were over twenty inches long. Thirteen of the fourteen trout were caught on Cowboy—my great attractor.

The evening prior to writing this article I called Pat Hogan, my friend who lives in Trempealeau County. Pat is a dyed-in-the-wool Panther Martin spin fisherman. However, after fishing with me this spring, he ordered some Mepps See Best spinners. Pat said, "Jay, we have had a lot of rain down here and the streams are muddy. But I was out yesterday on Beaver Creek, and I used your gold See Best lure. I caught seven nice brown trout where normally I wouldn't have caught a fish in that muddy water."

My immediate thought: "Cowboy rides again!"

I haven't found my "cowboy," the Mepps #3 See Best lure with a bright gold blade, in any store in Wisconsin. You will need to order it out of the catalog or by computer. Phone them at 715-623-2382, or go online: www.mepps.com.

I have no affiliation with Sheldon's Inc., Mepps Lure Company. My only purpose is to inform you of a lure that is a great attractor. This lure attracts trout because it's colorful and different. It's something new that trout have not seen. Once it's used extensively in this area I'll have to find another attractor. But isn't that the challenge of trout fishing—to continue experimenting and learning? Meanwhile, I'll ride with Cowboy.

Trout Fishing Changed His Life

Experience is the best teacher. Those that know their lake, their
river, catch the most fish. They know when and where to fish.
And they don't waste time fishing when the fish aren't home."
– Clarence "Simon" Schultz, Washburn, WI

I had read about Clarence "Simon" Schultz in a book by O.
Warren Smith, *One Man's River*, published by Bayfield Street
Publishing in Washburn. Then I had the good fortune of being introduced to "Simon" Schultz during a Trout Unlimited meeting. A
month later, on a cold day in March, I was sitting at the kitchen
table in the Schultz family home where he had grown up. I was
admiring his creation, a collection of over fifteen hundred original
trout flies Simon had tied and named.

It was obvious to me, and Simon, that his collection was probably a world record. Simon told me he had talked to an official at the
Freshwater Fishing Hall of Fame in Hayward. "They would like to
put my collection on display and exhibit it as a world record," he
explained. "However, I have to turn each fly in its plastic container
so they are all facing the same way and are horizontal. Jay, I have
some work left to do."

Fly fishing for Simon began with a chance meeting of O. Warren
Smith, a well-known minister and trout angler, on the Sioux River
in Bayfield County. It was a three-and-a-half-mile walk to the Big
Rock Pool, on the Sioux River, from the family home in Washburn.
During the Great Depression, at his mother's request, Simon often
walked to the river in an effort to help feed the large family of nineteen. With a strap attached to a gunnysack across his back for a
trout creel, a telescopic rod, and Colorado Spinner, Simon was on a
mission to catch a limit of trout. However, it was not going well for
the seventeen-year-old that bright summer day in 1937. Upon losing a good trout, he started to cuss. Behind him came a voice:
"What are you fishing with, Sonny?" The gentleman taking a break
from fishing introduced himself. "I had seen him often on the
river," Simon explained. "He was making coffee over an open fire.
My mind was to catch fish and get out of there, so I continued to
cuss as we talked fishing and drank coffee." The gentleman's name

was O. W. Smith, and he told Simon to meet him that evening at the Arcade Cafe in Washburn, and he would fix him up with a trout fishing outfit. Simon told his mother about meeting Smith and about the offer. His mother told Simon she knew O. W. Smith, and he was a minister. Simon told me how he had nervously paced around the kitchen table, the same table where we were sitting. He thought he would get a lecture on cussing rather than a fly fishing outfit. His mother encouraged him to go and meet the Reverend Smith at the cafe. Reluctantly, he went, and received not only a split bamboo fly rod but also a reel, line, net, creel, and trout flies.

Many of us over thirty can look back upon a singular event in life that had such an impact that it changed us forever. With the magic fly rod, Simon soon learned to tie flies, and his life would never be the same.

Simon taught many aspiring anglers how to tie flies and how to fish for trout. He became known as the premier trout angler in the region. Trout anglers new to the region contacted Simon and encouraged him to take them fishing. Simon said, "I was getting so many calls to take strangers fishing I decided to get a guide license and make some money. The first person I guided enjoyed the experience so much that he insisted on buying me a big dinner. When he asked what he owed, I couldn't charge him after he had bought dinner. When I got home my wife asked, 'Well, Simon, how much did you earn today?' Jay, that is the way the whole summer went. After they wined and dined me, I couldn't charge them. So I guided for one year and didn't make enough money to pay for my license. But I sure met some fine people."

Simon explained to me that he had fished all the trout-holding water on the Sioux River and every trout stream in Bayfield County. I asked, "How did you become so successful at catching trout?"

"First, experience is the best teacher. Those that know their lake, their river, catch the most fish. They know when and where to fish. And Jay, they don't waste time fishing when the fish aren't home. Second, it's all in the presentation of your bait. When they are hungry, anybody can catch them. If they don't hit, you try something different. They feed every day, so if they don't feed in the morning, you stay and fish evening."

Simon told me he still had the fly rod given to him by the Reverend Smith. I asked to see it. One month short of his eighty-second birthday, Simon stood straight and slender as he held the old split bamboo rod with soft hands. His clear, sky-blue eyes looked upon the magic rod with affection. The gift had changed his life. We both knew it.

MAGIC ROD - Clarence "Simon" Schultz, of Washburn, looks fondly at a fly rod he received as a gift in 1937 - a gift that changed his life forever.

Forty-Eight Degrees Is Normal for a Trout

The fifty-degree rise is a long held secret. And I'm hesitant to reveal it. However, if I have been doing a good job as a writer and sportsman, by now I should have convinced you of the need to release trout.

Have you ever taken the temperature of spring water? If you have, you know it is forty-eight degrees. It doesn't matter if you take the temperature of spring water in northern or southern Wisconsin, in January or July; it's a consistent forty-eight degrees.

I'm convinced that most trout would migrate to spring water in winter if it were readily available. Northlanders who in the fall migrate to Florida or Arizona we call "snowbirds." What should we call trout that travel upstream to the warm headwaters in fall? Let's call them spawners, because that is really what they are. "Snowbirds" don't go south to have children. In fact, some may go south to get away from the cold *and* the children.

We can manipulate our environment and increase our range of comfort. Today people can live year-round in both Death Valley and Antarctica. That is a temperature range of about two hundred degrees. The temperature range of trout is 33–73, only forty degrees.

So big deal. Forty-eight degrees is normal for trout—what does that mean? Trout are cold-blooded with a body temperature exactly the same as the water temperature. They feel comfortable at forty-eight degrees, and will begin to feed as the water temperature rises above that level. The opposite takes place when the temperature begins to drift down below forty-eight degrees. So, ideally, what you want to do is fish when the temperature of the water is rising above forty-eight degrees. I call it the fifty-degree rise. This is a theory of mine; I don't think you will read this anywhere else, but I have solid evidence to support my theory. The theory works especially well in northern Wisconsin, where streams run consistently cold. For example, I have found summer (June through August) temperatures in Bayfield County, on the Flag, Cranberry, Sioux, and Fish Creek, to be 53–56 degrees—colder than most Wisconsin trout streams. When you know the average temperature of the stream, it makes it easy for you to hit the fifty-degree rise and avoid the forty-eight degree drop.

I can't emphasize this too much—*trout are very sensitive to water temperature change.* Even a change of only two degrees can make a big difference. But that shouldn't seem unusual, because we notice it too. To feel comfortable, we raise or lower the thermostat. For trout, it often means the difference between feeling good and really going on a feeding binge, or feeling uncomfortable and not eating.

Consistency results in predictability. Since our temperatures are more consistent in the summer, it makes it easy to predict when to fish trout. The fifty-degree rise happens consistently just about every morning in the summer. Therefore: *in the summer, fish mornings.* Once I started taking the temperature of the water every time I went trout fishing, and compared that to the catch; it was easy for me to figure out when to fish trout.

The fifty-degree rise is a long-held secret. And I'm hesitant to reveal it. However, if I have been doing a good job as a writer and sportsman, by now I should have convinced you of the need to release trout. I plan on continuing to give you secrets, so please release trout and have the thrill of watching them swim away.

Last year, when I fished early morning, I was able to hit the fifty-degree rise from June to September. My best fishing, in terms of fish per hour, was on two of those streams I listed above. (By the way, the statistics I give you are from the note card and pen I carry on the stream and then enter into my journal.) On June 13, I fished from 7:40 a.m. to 11:25 a.m. It was a cloudy day, so I had success fishing later in the morning than usual. When I started at 7:40 a.m., the water and air temperature were both fifty degrees. As the air temperature went up to sixty degrees, the water temperature took a slow rise. The fish were in a feeding frenzy. I caught and released seventeen trout, from nine to twenty-three inches.

September 19—actually a bit late in the year for a morning fifty-degree rise—I fished from 7:15 a.m. to 9:15 a.m. I caught and released sixteen trout, from nine to fifteen inches. Catching and releasing sixteen trout in two hours is as good as it gets. Most of your time is spent hooking, playing, and releasing fish. The water temperature was fifty-four degrees, and the air sixty-six. The water temperature was rising on a cloudy morning with a few sprinkles of rain. It seemed like all the fish in the stream were hitting.

I went back to that same stream on September 27 and fished just upstream from where I had fished on September 19. I fished from 7:40 a.m. to 9:40 a.m., and caught one eleven-inch trout. The air temperature was forty-two degrees, and that caused a drop in water temperature below normal, to forty-five degrees. The trout were uncomfortable and refused to hit anything I presented.

Temperature, more than anything else, tells trout when to feed. The next time you grill steak, and you put on a jacket to be comfortable because the temperature dropped below forty-eight degrees, think about it—if you were a trout, you wouldn't eat.

Dangers of Walking on the Wild Side

Immediately, I decided to fish trout and waded into the stream.
The big bear slowly and deliberately circled me, while grunting to
complain about my entering its domain. The more encounters you
have with bear, the more you learn to respect their space.

The first fundamental of catching large trout, or a lot of trout, is to fish where and when others don't fish. Following the first fundamental will get you into some wild country at least half a mile away from the nearest bridge. The most heavily fished area, and usually the least dangerous to fish, is within one half mile upstream and downstream from the nearest bridge. If you get into trouble near the bridge, someone is likely to hear your call for help.

When you walk a trout stream, I believe it's best to stay in the stream. If you walk the bank, it's easier to scare the fish, and you may step into a beaver hole. A sudden drop into a hole can result in a sprained ankle, twisted knee, pulled back muscle, or broken leg.

In the Lake Superior region, you can get into trouble by failing to read clay deposits in the streambed, though I consider that less of a hazard than walking the bank. I have come close to getting stuck in clay on the Cranberry, Flag, White, Long Branch, and Iron Rivers. Once you begin to sink into clay, back off immediately—the next step could get you mired and unable to move. Last year, on April 27, when fishing the middle section of the Cranberry River, I saw a pair of hip boots stuck in a clay bank. Then I noticed a pair of socks on top of the bank. I concluded that a young angler had failed to read that bank of clay and walked into it. Unable to free the hip boots, he or she backed out in stocking feet. Yes, I will check to see if the hip boots are still there. No, I will not try to fetch them.

Where I fish, in wild country, I am often more likely to see a bear track than the track of an angler. The black bear is a danger, particularly a sow bear in spring with cubs. Early one Saturday morning in May, twenty years ago, I was walking down an old logging road to fish Log Creek in Sawyer County. When I rounded a curve, I saw, one hundred yards in front of me, a large bear chase three cubs up a pine tree next to the road. I turned and walked back to my vehicle. I decided to fish another stream.

The year before, a bear had taught me to respect its space. I was on a wild venture, walking more than an hour into the Bibon Marsh to fish the Long Branch. Suddenly, in the thick tag elders next to the stream, scarcely thirty yards away, I heard a bear grunt. Immediately, I decided to fish trout and waded into the stream. The big bear slowly and deliberately circled me, while grunting to complain about my entering its domain. The more encounters you have with bear, the more you learn to respect their space.

A trout fisherman fishing wild country told about being followed by a big black bear. He assumed the bear smelled the brook trout in his creel. One by one, the bear was given the trout, and the fisherman walked out with an empty creel.

On rare occasions, a black bear will come at you. Then it's best not to run, but to stand and face the bear and demonstrate you are not easy prey. From information I have gathered, the evidence seems clear that it is better to use pepper spray to ward off a bear than a firearm. The bear will immediately turn and run when sprayed in the face with pepper spray. If you use a firearm, you may wound the bear and put yourself in a precarious position.

Hornets are a danger I have frequently encountered along trout streams. When only five, I was walking the bank following Dad, who was wading the stream. Hidden in the tall grass was a hornets' nest. I walked into it, and the angry hornets got me three times before I reached Dad, yelling and crying. Dad got stung a couple times as he beat the hornets off with his hat. As long as I continued to walk stream banks, I managed to walk into hornets' nests and get stung. However, the danger doesn't end there. Fishing the Long Branch three years ago, while reaching to lift a branch out of the way, I saw an unfamiliar shape out of the corner of my eye. I turned and looked into the eyes of two impatient hornets sitting on the side of their nest. Slowly I lowered my hand, bid the hornets good day, and waded around the branch.

We may have more dangers to deal with today than in the past. Lyme Disease is a danger I didn't have for most of my life. Today, I often avoid contact with wood and deer ticks by using chest-high waders and always wading the stream. A necessary precaution is to always take a shower and check for ticks after trout fishing or walking in an area likely to contain ticks.

With caution, experience, and knowledge, you can avoid stepping in a beaver hole, getting stuck in clay, a close encounter with a bear, and getting stung by hornets. However, I still manage to get temporarily turned around in wild country. That is why I never go fishing without a compass. Getting lost is not good—it's a waste of fishing time.

And that is another story.

All Things Change, Including Trout Anglers

The angler at [The Sportsman's Stage] no longer has to catch fish to find satisfaction. Often he is strongly motivated to teach and to become a mentor. He finds satisfaction in introducing or coaching others in the sport.

– Dr. Robert Jackson, UW-La Crosse

Even nature, which we view as fairly constant, changes out of necessity. This year, due to the invasion of tent caterpillars, trees in the northland leafed out again in July. Without some understanding of the cause, this would certainly have been confusing.

It's probably not so much nature as it is people that cause confusion. Confusion, for example, when they are acting out of the ordinary. When a child acts too mature. When an adult acts too childish.

We go through stages of development—child, adolescent, young adult, middle age, and senior. And we expect people of each age group to act accordingly. However, isn't it fun to sometimes act out of character—out of age? I find the senior who will occasionally act like a child or adolescent to be an entertaining person. He or she is less inhibited, less formal, someone I often enjoy being around.

I believe one should enjoy every stage of development along the journey of life. To do so, we may have to occasionally slip forward, or backward, to experience that stage from a different perspective.

By now you're beginning to wonder, where is this guy going? What I'm leading up to is this: trout anglers go through stages of development—stages of evolution. And that evolution, that development, has been researched and documented. The stages of trout fishing are not unlike our stages of maturity. However, with trout fishing it is more of an evolution than a human development, and it's therefore less predictable.

The late Dr. Robert Jackson, of the University of Wisconsin-La Crosse, researched the evolution of the trout angler. He published his results in the June/July 1989 issue of *Wisconsin Outdoor Journal*. Dr. Jackson titled his article "Evolution of a Trout Fisherman."

When researching angler characteristics, Bob Jackson realized there were certain developmental stages that were characteristic, and somewhat unique, to trout anglers. A previous research study done by Dr. James Henshall, a physician and angler, identified three stages of development. Dr. Jackson's study began where Henshall left off. He identified five developmental stages: confirming, through additional research, Dr. Henshall's three stages of development, and adding two more stages.

Henshall suggested Stage One is wanting to catch fish—to limit out. Stage Two is catching a trophy. And Stage Three is when catching fish is more important than how many or how big.

After ten years of research, Jackson added a new Stage One as well as a Stage Five to Henshall's list. Stage One is a "how does it work" phase. This is when the angler wants to master the basics of casting—presenting the lure. Jackson said similar phases could be found in learning about photography, shooting, and canoeing. Dr. Jackson called his added fifth stage, that evolves beyond Henshall's list, "The Sportsman's Stage." Jackson wrote: "The angler at this stage no longer has to catch fish to find satisfaction. Often he is strongly motivated to teach and to become a mentor. He finds satisfaction in introducing or coaching others in the sport. Actually catching fish or battling a trophy never loses its attraction, but the sportsman-stage trouter confesses that he may spend more time watching trout rise or studying moving water than in fishing."

You can compare this to the stages of life. However, as I said, the stages of trout angling are more evolutionary. I knew the late Bob Jackson as a college professor, an excellent fly fisherman, and an active member of Trout Unlimited; he was a knowledgeable trout angler in addition to being skilled at research. As a part of his study, Dr. Jackson interviewed nine hundred Wisconsin trout anglers. He found that about half of the Trout Unlimited members began fishing trout after their twenty-second birthday—as young adults. Taking up the sport this late suggested that the angler specialized in a particular method and was further along in the five stages of development.

One part of Dr. Jackson's study was to interview a group of about a dozen experienced trout anglers. I was a member of the group, and I recall the members of the group were all male and about forty to fifty years of age. Most of us were probably in the fourth or fifth stage of trout angler evolution. Bob Jackson asked us about the satisfaction we found in trout fishing. Our responses in general were enjoyment of nature, just being out-of-doors, appreciating the beauty of trout, solitude, and using our fishing skills.

Of course, you can ask yourself what stage of trout fishing evolution you're in. However, the stage is not as important as your enjoyment of the sport. The neat thing about trout fishing is you need not fear moving to the next stage, because you can revert back to an earlier stage whenever you want to. You can pretend to do that in life—but it's only pretend, because there is no denying the aging process. However, isn't it those who occasionally pretend that have the most fun?

The angler in stage five finds satisfaction in teaching others how to fish.

World Traveling Trout Angler

It's wild country, where we thought trout had never seen an imitation... You could see fish holding in a feeding position. It's thrilling to see that fish come up to the surface and take a fly that matches the insects they are feeding on. It's the pinnacle of trout fishing.

—Dick Berge, Iron River, WI

We talked in his office, his trout chamber, his fly tying room par excellence. He had recently returned from a two-week trout fishing trip to Argentina. Five years ago, Dick Berge had chased trout in New Zealand. Prior to that, he had fished trout in Ontario and British Columbia. Quite unusual, I thought, for someone raised on a farm near Valders, Wisconsin. He had not been close to a trout stream, and was therefore unable to fish trout until he had wheels at age sixteen. Now, the big difference between the angler at age sixteen and the man retired in his sixties is the circle of his travels and the perfection of his skill at tying trout flies. The Dick Berge from Valders traveled on a gas tank half-full. The Dick Berge from Deep Lake, in Bayfield County, ties perfect imitations of insects he sells to keep his tank full and pay for his travels.

In 1995, Dick and his wife Eve built their retirement home facing Deep Lake, southwest of Iron River, in Bayfield County. Both Eve and Dick retired from school teaching in Madison, Wisconsin.

When I asked Dick why he went fishing in Argentina, he smiled, his eyes twinkled, and he said, "Years ago I read about Joe Brooks fishing trout in Argentina and saw pictures of the big fish he caught. Jay, that trip was the fulfillment of a dream."

Along with Bill Heart, owner of Heart Graphics in Ashland, and three friends from Madison, Dick Berge left for Argentina on January 2 and returned to Wisconsin on January 18. Southern Cross Outfitters made all the arrangements for lodging, meals, transportation, guides, and so forth. Dick said the accommodations and the fishing were excellent. They fished some of the best rivers and lakes in northern Patagonia. They were in the foothills of the Andes, similar to some areas in Wyoming and Montana. I asked Dick if the fishing was about the same as he found in our Rocky

Mountain region. "It's better there than in our western states because it's relatively undiscovered. It's kind of like it was about fifty years ago fishing trout in Wyoming or Montana. And in Argentina they are protecting the resource because it's catch-and-release."

The outfitter gave the anglers a list of fly rods, lines, and flies to bring to Argentina. Although the trip was well planned, Dick knew from other trips to bring along a fly tying kit. He explained, "Trout rise to flies not on the list—it happens all the time."

Three days were spent on a float trip down a river considerably larger than our Brule. Long casts were needed with seven- and eight-weight rods to reach the pocket water and edges where big fish were holding. They used weighted lines with large number four and two woolly bugger flies. The flies imitated thick round-bodied poncara crabs that big brown and rainbow trout were eating. Rounding a bend in the river, they were as likely to see a mountain lion (called puma in Argentina) as another angler.

Although they caught brook trout to twenty inches in mountain lakes, plus rainbow and brown in the rivers to twenty-four inches, it was not necessarily the excellent fishing that Dick thought would make a lasting impression. He talked about the scenery. About the colorful *gaucho* (cowboy) herding horses. He mentioned the perfect summer weather in the southern hemisphere of seventy to eighty degrees, with sunshine every day. "But," he said, "I'll always remember the friendliness of the people. They wanted to practice their English on us. They were so warm, so anxious to please. If anything, too anxious."

"What do you mean too anxious?" I inquired.

"Bill Heart and I had a guide to ourselves and he was excellent—but he was always there. He didn't understand we were from northern Wisconsin—that we had fished wild country and knew how to take care of ourselves. He didn't know we liked to explore, try some of our own techniques, and fish a stream on our own." Dick stopped tying a fly, looked at me, smiled, and continued. "Bill and I hatched a plan to slip away early in the morning and sneak up the Rio Pichi-Leufu to fish a canyon area. It's wild country, where we thought trout had never seen an imitation. The Rio Pichi-Leufu is beautiful, flowing over gravel and around large boulders—it's crystal-clear snowmelt water from the Andes. We were sight-fishing for large brown trout. You could see the fish holding in a feeding position. It's just thrilling to see that fish come up to the surface and take a fly that matches the insects they are feeding on. It's the pinnacle of trout fishing. We were catching and releasing heavy brown trout to twenty-four inches. Jay, it's a fly fisherman's dream come true. There we were, wading upstream in that canyon on the Rio Pichi-Leufu for two hours before the guide caught up with us." Dick laughed. "Kind of like two kids skipping school."

Raining Supreme on Trout Streams

*When a front moves in and produces a light, misty rain, go
fishing. Under this low light condition, trout are likely to hit
all day long.*

It has always amazed me that most people wait for the good
weather days to go fishing. It seems comfort, rather than catching
fish, is their prime consideration.

If you want to catch large trout, the two most important items
you own may not be your rod and reel. By the time you finish this
article, you should understand the importance of owning a rain
gauge and a good-quality rain suit.

The last large brown trout I caught and kept came from the
South Fork of Beaver Creek in Trempealeau County. You can step
across the creek and get only one foot wet. I fished the small
stream on Memorial Day, May 31, 1982. Usually, I never fish on a
holiday after anglers have been on the stream scaring trout.
However, my rain gauge said the rain that had come down on
Sunday night had been a one-half inch rainfall.

The stream was slightly discolored; worms, crickets, and ants
had washed into the creek. The twenty-four-inch brown trout was
feeding at the head of the pool. With a cloudy morning, and the turbidity in the stream providing cover, she felt comfortable leaving
the logjam at the tail of the pool. Conditions were perfect that
Memorial Day morning for catching large trout.

The first rain observation: Whenever there is about a one-half
inch rainfall at night, go fishing early the following morning. Don't
guess—buy a rain gauge. If you know where a large trout is holding, and it is a low-light, cloudy morning, you have an excellent
chance of catching the fish for the wall. A trout becomes large by
hiding, being a recluse, and only coming out to feed when food is
readily available and there is turbidity—silting of the water—to provide cover.

The second rain observation: During a light misty rain, you
should go fishing. And this observation works not only for trout but
for musky, walleye, and crappie as well. In my trout journal, I have
numerous entries of both catching and losing large trout during a
light misty rain.

I was wearing waders and a Gore Tex rain jacket on a cool misty morning in June 1992, when wading up Fish Creek in Bayfield County. A large steelhead came out from under the bank in a corner pool and smashed my spinner. The steelhead immediately exploded into the air, then made a strong run to the tail of the pool, and shook the lure like a dog shaking a rag doll. Another run upstream with more powerful shaking, and the lure worked loose. It was gone. I recorded in my journal, "About 30 inches long and real heavy—definitely a wall-hanger."

When a front moves in and produces a light, misty-type rain, go fishing. Under this low light condition, trout are likely to hit all day long.

Third rain observation: Go trout fishing three days after a downpour of more than one inch. Fish early morning, and you will find trout at the head of the pool, feeding with a vengeance. For many years, I didn't fish trout for a week or more after a heavy rain. I missed some great fishing opportunities. A heavy rain, of more than one inch, will wash food not only into the stream, but also out, away from the trout. A high, fast-moving stream will cause trout to use more energy to maintain position in the stream, resulting in the need for more food.

One word of caution: never fish during a thunderstorm. By the time you see lightning or hear thunder, trout have quit feeding and taken cover. You should immediately quit fishing and head for home.

All three observations work well for brown trout. And I have discovered, since living in the northland, that fishing on a misty morning will practically guarantee success when you know where a large steelhead is lurking.

Some misty morning, I'll see you on the stream.

Where to Fish the Stream

*Generally, the deepest water with cover is found in the middle
third of the stream. So if the gravel beds are also in the middle
third, you have the best combination for large trout.*

Let's suppose that you plan to fish a trout stream you were told
is a good stream. However, you have never fished the stream and
don't have a clue where to begin fishing.

We'll use the North Fork of Fish Creek, in Bayfield County, as
the imaginary stream. Before we begin, I must tell you I am writing
in generalities—each stream is unique, and that is a quality that
makes exploring streams exciting.

Prior to wetting a line, I take out a map and divide the stream
into thirds. For this exercise I use a topographic map, a county
map, or the *Wisconsin Atlas and Gazetteer.* Since the North Fork is
about eighteen miles long, each third will be around six miles in
length.

You will usually find the best pools in the middle third. As the
stream gathers runoff in its course, it tends to erode the banks in
the middle and upper thirds. When the gradient decreases, in the
lower third, sand and sediment carried by the stream is deposited.
Thus you will usually find the lower third to be wide and flat, lacking depth and cover. However, if there is structure in the lower third
it can create a large pool—often the best pool on the stream.
Structure may result from an abandoned bridge, a logjam, a cliff, a
rockslide, or trees causing a meander. Most fishermen are not
inclined to walk a long distance to fish one large pool. My advice:
find the structure and large pool in the lower one-third of the
stream if you want to catch a large trout. Big trout like seclusion,
and you are likely to find one in the lower third that is seldom
fished in July and August.

If you plan to fish the North Fork of Fish Creek early or late in
the season, you need additional information that you cannot possibly get from a map. You need to find the gravel beds—the spawning area for steelhead early, and brown trout late.

Generally, the deepest water with cover is found in the middle
third of the stream. So, if the gravel beds are also in the middle
third, you have the best combination for large trout. Fish Creek has

some excellent gravel beds for spawning in the middle third of the stream. The middle third is both above and below Fish Creek Road. (Reminder: the area above Fish Creek Road is closed until the first Saturday in May.) In the middle third of Fish Creek, I have caught and released brown trout to twenty-one inches, and steelhead to twenty-seven inches.

Once you discover the gravel beds in a stream, you need to determine specifically the best beds within that section of trout stream. For example, on Fish Creek, within a quarter mile of where I lost a steelhead which I estimated to be thirty inches long, I have caught and released other large steelhead. I discovered there are very special spawning areas where fish return year after year to spawn. The gravel seems to be just the right consistency. The pool below the gravel bed has cover for protection. These special secret places, where you regularly find large steelhead in the spring and brown trout in the fall, you must bank in the lock box of your mind. Don't leave a forked stick in the sandbar where you rest your pole. Don't leave an old folding chair at the big pool below the gravel bed. However, I am considering including in my will some of the hot spots I have discovered. Not all the hot spots—I wouldn't deprive my ancestors the joy of discovery.

A 27 inch steelhead caught on Fish Creek in a pool below a gravel bed.
Those special secret places are banked in the lock box of your mind.

95

Brook Trout for Breakfast

*We caught and released seven small trout for every nine-inch trout
we kept. Al said his stream had a limited food supply, and it was
important to keep trout to eat. There was not enough food to
enable the trout to grow more than twelve inches long.*

Al called. "Are you coming out to fish trout in the morning?"
"Yes," I responded. "Is it OK if I meet you at your place about six?"
"Plan to eat breakfast here. We'll have brook trout for breakfast."
"Brook trout for breakfast! I've never had brook trout for breakfast."
"I was out this evening and caught five. Be here at six for breakfast."
I hung up, turned to my wife, and said, "Albin Polkoski is cooking breakfast—brook trout. I haven't had brook trout since our trip
to Montana, eleven years ago."
Brook trout are a meal fit for a king. But even a king couldn't
order up a meal of wild brook trout in the heat of summer.
We would be fishing the headwaters of Al's stream. It's a cold
spring creek, part of the Iron River system in Bayfield County. His
active Brittany spaniel was leading the way to the creek that warm
morning in late July. I was riding on the ATV behind Al. The trail
narrowed, and Al steered between big trees with scarcely a
whisker's breadth between the Polaris and the poplar. I held my rod
tight in one hand and gripped the ATV with the other as we slowly
descended the hill to park beside cold water running over gravel.
Albin Polkoski, at age seventy-nine, had been fishing trout for
seventy-five years. Spike, Al's dog, was the first to hit the water. He
was happily splashing down the creek in front of us, scaring all the
trout. I silently asked, "How did Al catch breakfast fishing with this
dog?"
After fishing downstream for fifteen minutes, Al suggested we
fish upstream above a series of beaver dams. He called Spike and
told him to sit. Spike was wet and satisfied as he sat next to Al and
watched every cast.
We caught and released seven small trout for every nine-inch
trout we kept. Al said his stream had a limited food supply, and it
was important to keep trout to eat. There was not enough food to
enable the trout to grow more than twelve inches long.

Al had been trapping beaver for years to keep the population under control and protect the gravel spawning areas. As I was fishing upstream above the second beaver dam, it occurred to me that Albin Polkoski keeps a close watch on his stream. I listened to the cold fifty-eight-degree water gurgling over beaver sticks, sealed with rock and mud to form the dam, and I kept repeating Johnny Cash's lyrics: "I keep a close watch on this heart of mine." Only I changed the words to, "Al keeps a close watch on this stream of his."

We were fishing about ten miles above the Orienta Dam that had prevented migration of fish upstream from Lake Superior. A steelhead or coaster brook trout had not been swimming here since the dam was constructed. And the DNR plans to install a fish barrier when the dam is removed this year. So Al's stream does not have, and will not have, coaster brook trout swimming in the cold clear water.

After landing my third keeper, a bright-colored ten-inch male, I thought there must be other people keeping a close watch on their steam. Their stream that flows barrier-free to Lake Superior and still has a run of coaster brook trout. And because, like Al, they were limiting access, they had protected the rare and diminishing coaster brook trout. The ten-inch brook trout jumped inside my basket— had I known it to be a coaster, I would have released it.

The coaster is a brook trout known for its travels to and from Lake Superior. It is to the brook trout what the steelhead is to the rainbow. But even a fishery biologist can't distinguish the difference between a brook trout and a coaster. And since the coaster is in danger of becoming extinct in Wisconsin, it's a no-brainer, isn't it? Anglers should, until we have more specific information, release brook trout caught in Lake Superior and in all streams flowing barrier-free into Lake Superior.

I proceeded above the next beaver dam and immediately landed my fourth and fifth keeper. I walked back across the dam and downstream in time to get a picture of Al landing brook trout number five. Spike had been sitting quietly in the tall grass until Al brought the trout out of the water. Then he began jumping with excitement as if to say, "Way to go, Master!"

Back at Al's house, I was on the tailgate taking off my waders. I knew his wife had passed away about four years ago. We talked about his new family member, Spike. It was apparent to both Al and me that Spike had a hunter's nose and instinct. He responded well to Al's commands and we both, naturally, thought about grouse hunting.

That evening I rolled the trout in corn meal and fried them crisp in olive oil. My wife and I enjoyed a meal fit for a king. I told Diana about my fishing experience with Al and Spike. Then I nodded my head and said exactly what we were both thinking: "I'm really a lucky man."

Hot Spots for Large Brown Trout

Although big browns are sometimes caught in famous pools, it is likely they were just passing through. A large brown trout likes seclusion, and fishing pressure will soon force it to leave and search for privacy.

Of our three kinds of stream trout (brook, brown, and rainbow), brown trout are the most elusive, secretive, intelligent, and difficult to catch. This article is written to help you find those areas where large brown trout hide—I define large brown trout as those over twenty inches in length—and therefore help you catch one for a picture or for the wall.

There are some famous pools where big fish are known to hold; for example, the pool on the Flag River, in Bayfield County, where the East and West Fork meet; and the Big Rock Pool on the Sioux River, in Bayfield County. Although big browns are sometimes caught in famous pools, it is likely they are just passing through. A large brown likes seclusion, and fishing pressure will soon force it to leave and search for privacy. If the brown trout were a human, it wouldn't live in Cook County, Illinois. It would find a hideout in a secluded area of Ashland, Iron, Sawyer, or Bayfield County.

All trout need cover for protection. Brown trout have an affinity for cover dense enough to provide continuous shade. They will seek out the north-facing cliff, or north- facing steep bank with trees that block out the sun. They never want to come out into the sun when chasing a meal. Find that pool seldom fished, that has cover where the sun never shines, and you have found a hideout for a large brown trout.

One of the largest browns I have seen in a trout stream was in the La Crosse River, in Monroe County. Early in the morning on July 30, 1986, I was fishing upstream, on public grounds, near Fort McCoy. I recorded in my journal, "Saw one very large trout—estimate 8 pounds and 28 inches. Must return for it. It was in feeding position, in bumpy water, in middle of stream above a bank with cover. It turned and went back along the bank downstream to cover." I returned, but never saw the fish. Having been discovered, it may have left for a hiding place with more privacy.

Since that experience in 1986, I have caught a number of large browns from bumpy water. Bumpy water can result from logs and rocks in the stream, or when the stream narrows and drops fast. It often results in a narrow deep-water area with small rapids that provides protection from predators.

In a stream with brook, brown, and rainbow, the brown trout will dominate the areas of cover provided by logs. Always fish carefully the deep pools (especially those with continuous shade) that contain logs for cover.

Continuous shade can be provided by debris (in the form of grass, leaves, sticks, and so on) floating on the water. I caught a twenty-one-inch brown on the Long Branch of the White River hiding beneath debris. A floating log and some tag alders caught and held debris floating down the river. I cast across the stream and was allowing my spinner to make a loop beneath the debris when the feisty brown hit.

I seek out black willow trees when fishing a trout stream. If the black willow is on a corner, the stream will hollow out the bank beneath the tree. The mature willow arching across the stream provides continuous cover. Six years ago, prior to my move to Bayfield County, I found a large brown when fishing Rush Creek. Rush Creek, one of my favorite trout streams, is in Crawford County, south of La Crosse, Wisconsin. I was fishing the lower third of the stream. It was a long walk to a secluded area seldom fished. I noticed a huge black willow upstream on a corner. In my haste to wade up to the black willow hole, I spooked a large trout I estimated to be twenty-six inches long. The big brown swam back into hiding beneath the roots of the willow. Preparing to move, and knowing I wouldn't soon return to fish Rush Creek, I informed my fishing friend Bob Miller. Bob called a month later and said, "Jay, that brown in the black willow pool is larger than you thought. It will go at least twenty-eight inches. I had it on but couldn't hold it out from the roots of that black willow!"

Big brown trout with a preference for depth, cover, shade, and seclusion always find a hideout. Another big brown will take over the black willow pool on Rush Creek. Maybe I should pack for a trip to Crawford County.

A Trout's Eye View

A trout can see objects to the side independently with the use of one eye. He can improve his vision by concentrating both eyes to see things in front or above him. An otter knows a trout's blind spot is behind and below him.

All trout must avoid bright light. Our eyes can adjust to light; the eyes of a trout can't adjust. Without getting too technical, I want to point out the difference between the human eye and the eye of trout. Then you will understand why it's best to fish in low light conditions. Also, you will know why you should present your lure, and move about, in the blind spot of the trout.

We can control the amount of light entering the eye by changing the diameter of the pupil. It takes a few minutes for your pupil to adjust when you come out of a movie theater on a sunny afternoon. A trout can't dilate the pupil to make an adjustment. Also, fish do not have eyelids, like we do, to partially close and help avoid the uncomfortable bright light. When you look at the pupil of a trout, you will notice it is large in diameter. Their pupils admit all the light in their surroundings and this is the reason trout must avoid brightly lit areas. It is more difficult (indeed it must be painful) for a trout to come out from a dark undercut bank than it is for us to come out of the dark theater. Big trout are proportionately more sensitive to light than small trout. Big trout will not come out into the sunlight. When the sun is out, your lure must enter their dark domain.

August 4, 2000, I started wading upstream at 6:10 a.m., fishing my "secret stream." It was a warm, cloudless morning. By 7:55, just one hour and forty-five minutes after I made my first cast, I had landed and released six brown trout, from eleven to nineteen inches. In the next hour, I caught only one trout, a nine-inch brown. As the day got brighter, the big trout shut down. Sure, I could have caught more trout if I had kept fishing, but they would have been small and far between. Since most anglers don't understand that the eye of the trout cannot handle bright light, they are not on the stream until after 8:00 a.m. in the summer months, and therefore average only two trout per day.

Trout have a higher ratio of rods to cones than human beings. Cones are needed to provide visual acuity in well-lighted areas. With more rods, that provide vision under low light conditions, big trout are natural low-light predators.

The first rule of trout fishing is to keep out of sight. If you look closely at the eyes of a trout, and most fish for that matter, you will notice that the fish can see both right and left at the same time. With eyes at the side of the head, they have better peripheral vision than we do.

Although some students believe teachers have eyes behind their head, in truth the human being has a rear blind spot that exceeds their forward area of vision. The human being can compensate for the blind spot by turning the head—something a trout can't do.

A trout can see objects to the side independently with the use of one eye. He can improve his vision by concentrating both eyes to see things in front of or above him. As the otter knows, a trout's blind spot is behind and below him. To protect the blind spot below him, a trout lurks at the bottom of the pool.

If you fish the early season (March to April), or late season (October to November), in those streams flowing into Lake Superior, you may find large trout out from under cover in the sunlight. The sun is lower in the atmosphere, and the rays of the sun are at an indirect angle. It's something trout can handle. Even then, however, brown trout will usually be under cover, because they are more likely to be more wary of danger than the other species. It's steelhead and brook trout that may be found feeding and languishing in the sunlight.

Remember, trout face into the current to watch for food and to maintain their position.

I have spent fifty years fishing upstream behind trout in their blind spot. Experts disagree on exactly how large the blind spot is behind a trout. However, all agree that it is considerably smaller than our blind spot. From my observations, I believe it is about sixty degrees: thirty degrees to the left of center and thirty to the right of center. When you are in that rear zone, a trout cannot see you. The trout, like you, has a fringe area where movement can be seen but not identified. If you are motionless in the fringe area, about fifteen degrees to the left or right of the blind spot, a trout will not identify you as a threat.

To consistently catch trout, fish when sunlight isn't on the water. Wade upstream and make your presentation from their blind spot. When you approach an area where a trout will be holding, move slowly and enjoy the experience—you will be rewarded.

SHADOW FISH - A trout can't dilate the pupil of the eye like we can and they do not have an eyelid. Therefore, they lurk in the dark shadows.

Secret Fish Holding Places

"Fish where and when others don't fish" is a basic tenet in all fishing. This basic tenet is more important today than it was over fifty years ago. In the pre-shopping mall era, people knew how to walk.

It really doesn't matter what kind of fish you are after. Sooner or later, if you fish often, you will find your own special fish-holding place. And if you want to continue to catch fish in that special place, you had best keep it a secret.

Cliff Dahl, a trout fisherman from Amasa, in the Upper Peninsula of Michigan, was known around town for catching large brook trout. He told me he actually had to quit fishing evenings and sneak out of town before daylight, or he would have someone following him. "How did you know someone was following?" I asked.

"Sometimes I saw them following, or I saw the dust trail in my rearview mirror on the gravel road. Whenever I thought someone was trailing me, I never went to my secret stream. I fished another trout stream."

Only about one out of four trout streams are worth fishing. Most don't have the water capacity to support large fish. I seldom fish a stream less than four miles long. Small streams, of a size you can jump across, usually lack the water volume and food production necessary for trout over fifteen inches long.

When it comes to finding those great fish-holding areas, it's a matter of elimination. Ninety percent of the water in a stream or lake doesn't hold fish. So you need to concentrate on ten percent of the water in the lake or stream. If you are fishing musky, it is even more selective. Max Michaelson, the musky expert on my fishing trip to Lake of the Woods in July 2001, said less than one percent of the water in a lake will hold muskies. So to find a large musky, you have to figure out how to eliminate ninety-nine percent of the water. Then musky fishing becomes a lot like trout fishing. To catch a large fish, you have to fish an area that has had little fishing pressure. Or fish the time of year, or time of day, when there is very little fishing pressure. On some heavily fished lakes and streams, the anglers that fish in the summer months need to fish after dark to have success. Examples are Grindstone Lake near Hayward and the Brule River in Douglas County.

The process of elimination is considerably less complicated for the trout angler than the musky fisherman.

If your desire is to catch small fish, often planters with rounded tails from brushing against concrete trout hatchery walls, fish near the bridge. Here it comes, my broken record scenario—to catch large trout, you have to walk ten minutes or more away from the bridge. "Fish where and when others don't fish" is a basic tenet in all fishing. This basic tenet is more important today than it was over fifty years ago. In the pre-shopping mall era, people knew how to walk. Today most people want drive-up or drive-through shopping.

When you translate that into fishing, you find more people fishing out of high-powered boats. And fewer anglers are walking trout streams. As a result, quality fishing in lakes is declining and stream fishing is improving.

With experience, you learn that some holding areas are better during one particular time of the year. My wife and I found good crappie ice fishing in an area on Eagle Lake, in the Township of Delta, southeast of Iron River. Diana and I tried fishing the area after ice-out but didn't find the crappies. It was good ice fishing for two years. Then other ice fishing anglers discovered the holding area and it has been poor fishing the last two years. My guess, it will return to quality fishing as fishing pressure dissipates. So we'll go back to check on the crappies again next winter.

I have four remote areas on four trout streams in northwest Wisconsin that I fish each year. The only thing they have in common is isolation. I seldom see a boot print, and have never met a trout angler while fishing those areas. Each of the areas has produced well for me in July through September. So, trout fishing friends, as the days grow shorter and the leaves turn color, it's time to take a map, a compass, some food, and something to drink, and walk into isolation, where you'll find trout that haven't seen a lure for weeks.

Each year, it seems, there are fewer anglers out there fishing those remote areas for trout. Most don't like to walk; they want drive-up fishing just like their shopping. If you see boot prints back in the wild, they could be mine.

Summer Fishing — Fish Early; Reminisce Late

Fish when the temperature is low and slowly rising. It happens like clockwork just about every morning in July and August.

During July and August, you don't have to wonder when the best time is to fish trout. For the warmest time of the year, you should fish during the coolest time of day. It's basically very simple. For warm days, fish during the coolest part of the day; and for cool days, fish during the warmest part of the day. Yet most anglers fail to grasp this basic concept. Maybe it's because they don't understand that fish are cold-blooded, their body temperature is exactly the same temperature of the water in which they swim.

I recall one particularly cold opener. The temperature had dropped well below freezing the first Saturday in May. Dad and I were fishing Grindstone Creek, southeast of Hayward, in Sawyer County. By eleven o'clock, we hadn't caught a trout, and I was ready to call it quits. Dad suggested we fish a trout pond next to the creek. A thin sheet of ice covered the south side of the pond. We moved immediately to fish in the sunshine, along the north shore that was free of ice. Dad, always the optimist, said the trout would soon feed as the water warmed. The theory that a degree or two in water temperature would turn trout on to feeding didn't seem reasonable to me, a young college student. About noon on that cold day in May, the water warmed a few degrees, and the brook trout started to hit. We caught some nice ten- to twelve-inch fish for a meal. Dad knew better than to listen to his college student son and quit fishing at eleven o'clock.

I learned a lot about the society of man in college. But the habits of trout were learned on trout streams. The direct experience lesson Dad taught me that cold day in May forty-six years ago was the first lesson in a chapter of temperature and trout. And I am still filling the chapter. Even as I write this, I am planning to develop a simple mathematical formula that will predict, anywhere in Wisconsin, the best time to fish trout on any particular day. (Those who remember me in high school math class know the formula will not be complicated.)

But for now, let's get back to summer trout fishing. The air temperature cools down all night, as a general rule, and is the lowest as the sun rises. This brings us to the first rule of summer fishing: Fish when the temperature is low and slowly rising. It happens like clockwork just about every morning in July and August.

The second rule of summer fishing is to fish during low light conditions. The summer sun is high in the sky and hitting the water almost directly during those warm summer days. A large trout won't come out into the bright sun to feed. So you must be on the stream early, or late, if you want to catch respectable fish over twelve inches long. In the evening, you will have less than two hours to fish as the water begins to cool down to a comfortable range for the trout. If you are on the water before sunrise, you will have at least three hours of good fishing before the sunshine hits more than half the water in the stream and the trout quit feeding.

The third rule of summer fishing: Trout learn not to feed when fishermen are on the stream. Early-morning anglers usually have the stream to themselves. How many people do you know get up at 4:00 a.m. so they can be on the water before the sun? By July, the trout know worm anglers show up at 9:00 a.m. and fly anglers begin to cast at 7:00 p.m. They train themselves to feed in the peace and quiet of early morning.

The fourth rule of summer fishing is that you can have more than three hours of excellent fishing. If you select a cloudy morning, a misty morning, or a morning with a light rain, you can have great fishing until noon.

The fifth rule of summer fishing is to leave the stream in time to get out of the woods before dark. I have had some near-tragic experiences by fishing late and trying to work my way out of the woods after dark. It just isn't safe to fish evenings in wild country and walk out of the woods after dark. You should fish early, and reminisce late.

If you have been reading my essays, you know the best trout fishing is a half-mile or more away from the nearest bridge or point of access. Like most adult people, adult trout like peace and quiet. Big trout are like wealthy people: they can take up residence wherever they want to. Only small trout live on Main Street. Which reminds me, isn't it easier to walk that half-mile, to where large trout live, when it's cool in early morning?

When Fishing, Don't Trust Woman with Magic Pole

It doesn't matter if you got the right equipment; it's all in how you use it.
— Diana Thurston, Viroqua, WI

Whenever we fish from a boat, it's expected that she will out-fish me. But trout fishing—that is my expertise; no way should my wife catch more trout than I.

Her pole is only five-and-a-half feet long, too short to qualify as a good spinning rod for underhand casting on small streams. For years, I have wanted to buy her a quality rod. "No!" she says. "My pole works just fine." At least she allows me to keep new line on her reel so she doesn't have a big fish break off.

In September, during her vacation, we went camping in west central Wisconsin. Our vacation site was a county campground at Nugget Lake in Pierce County. Although a busy campground on weekends, during the workweek we were the only campers.

We brought along a canoe and fished Nugget Lake. The lake is an impoundment of Plum Creek, a trout stream. The land around the lake, owned by the county, has remained wild and undeveloped. Close to the dam, we found forty feet of water and began fishing. Diana put on a chartreuse mini-mite jig. She immediately started hauling in big bluegills and crappies. I put on a mini-mite jig—no luck. It had to be the color, I thought, so I searched my tackle box and came up with a chartreuse jig. It helped; while she hauled in six large crappies and bluegills, I caught two. Diana couldn't cast as far as I, and it seemed to me she had a poor jigging technique. Must be that magic rod, I concluded.

The region surrounding Pierce County, in west central Wisconsin, has not been glaciated, and the spring water emerges from limestone bedrock. It's hard water, rich in nutrients, and it produces an abundance of food for forage fish and trout. The Rush River, in the center of the region, has produced more trout from ten to fifteen pounds than any other stream in Wisconsin, with the possible exception of the Brule. However, like the Brule, it is well known and heavily fished. My friend Pat Hogan fishes the region extensively, and he told me where to take Diana fishing on the Rush.

It had been more than five years since Diana had fished trout, so I instructed her on how to wade upstream and make the underhand flip cast with her yellow Panther Martin spinner. At first her casts were high, wild, and short. I just shook my head and said, "You should have listened to me and used the extra rod and reel I brought along for you. At least you're wearing my lightweight waders."

A couple hundred yards above the bridge, we came to a deep pool on a curve. However, there were tree limbs a few feet above the water, and it was a difficult cast. Being the good guide, I pointed out where she might be able to cast her lure between two branches. Somehow, with her magic rod, she made the impossible cast. A big brown immediately hit her lure. As I yelled, "Play the fish! Give it some line!" she reefed back on her magic rod and jerked it to the top of the water, where the fish repeatedly jumped. Not satisfied with reeling it in, she grabbed her line and hauled it in hand over hand. We measured that heavy, brightly colored Rush River brown trout. She had caught the largest fish of the day, a solid fifteen inches. Diana laughed, looked at her magic rod, and commented, "It doesn't matter if you got the right equipment; it's all in how you use it." She proudly held the big brown for a picture. In the instant that I snapped the shutter, the frantic fish jumped, hit the water wiggling, and swam away from the unorthodox woman angler. I got empty hands and a big smile for a picture.

The next day we fished the favorite stream of my friend Pat Hogan. He told me, "Jay, my secret stream has brown trout over twenty inches, and is loaded with native brook trout up to fourteen." In the first hole above the bridge, Diana caught and released a chunky nine-inch brook trout. In less than twenty-four hours, both her casting and ability to play a trout had made quantum leaps forward. We exchanged lead position each time we caught a trout. It was Diana's turn when we came to a deep rock-lined corner pool. She dropped her yellow Panther Martin spinner in the middle of the pool, let it settle to the bottom, and started to reel. The big brown hit, and she played the sixteen-inch fish like an expert. What a difference a day makes, I thought, as I snapped the picture.

Just as we were about to quit fishing I made a long cast to an undercut bank and caught a heavy seventeen-inch brown. Diana didn't say a word. But I thought I heard Dad's voice from above: "You darn near let a women beat you again!"

Diana Thurston holds a brown trout she caught with her magic pole. Her ability to catch nearly any kind of fish with her pole amazes her husband, the author.

When Less Js Better

I received lots of Christmas gifts as a child. But the only one I can recall is the BB gun. Whether we are talking about a Christmas gift or a trout stream, it's not the amount but the quality. Yes, less is often better.

Some of us, when we stop to think about it, know it is not "more," but often "less" that has given us life's memorable moments.

As a college student in the summer of 1957, I went west to Montana to work for the U.S. Forest Service. One weekend, three friends and I hiked eleven miles to fish a small stream on the western slope of a mountain range. We had the feeling we were the first to cast a fly upon the clear water of that little creek. We were fishing about a hundred yards apart, on small meanders in the valley of meadow grass and wild flowers between tall mountains. I yelled, "Just caught a cutthroat on a Black Gnat!"

Gary called back, "Caught a ten incher on a Royal Coachman."

Elliott responded, "They're hitting my Ginger Quill like mad!"

It didn't seem to matter what fly we used. I pulled off a weed seed and dropped it into the stream. It floated to the corner and a trout immediately rose to take it in.

We kept enough cutthroat trout to eat, and stopped fishing when we became tired of releasing those bright-colored cold-water trout.

I suppose it's still possible to find a stream in the United States that hasn't been fished. But one would probably have to hike in a remote mountain region of Alaska.

Prior to retiring and moving to Bayfield County, I worked for the School District of La Crosse as an elementary school principal. Sometimes I was able to fish evenings. However, most of my trout fishing was done on weekends. Then, in the 1980s, when we had evening parent-teacher conferences, we earned a Friday vacation day. Early one Friday in the spring of 1987, I was fishing Tainter Creek in Vernon County. I had a vision of having the stream to myself. However, before noon I had to share the stream with another angler. "What is he doing here?" I thought. "He should be working." Then I noticed the gray hair, and knew he was old enough to be retired.

Guess when I fish trout now—it's seldom on weekends. And it's usually early in the morning. When it comes to trout fishing and people, less is better.

What was the best Christmas gift you ever received? I was nine years old when Mother and Dad gave me my best present—a BB gun. They were telling me I was old enough to be trusted with a gun. I felt grown up. And Dad taught me how to act with a gun—to act grown up. I received lots of Christmas gifts as a child. But the only one I can recall is the BB gun.

Whether we are talking about a Christmas gift or a trout stream, it's not the amount but the quality. Yes, less is often better.

Monday, June 26, 2001, I was working as a volunteer west of Siren, Wisconsin, where a tornado had a week before caused destruction. I was part of a crew with chain saws cutting trees. We were helping elderly people who needed uprooted trees removed from their yards.

For most of the day, I was working alone in a front yard. One large poplar tree was leaning into a decorative cherry tree. About half the roots of the poplar were still attached. The branches and the stress from the bend in the trunk were holding the tree about seven feet off the ground. This was a "widow maker." I studied it for five minutes before I decided where I would carefully make my first cut. It sounded like a firecracker when the trunk flew up and the tree came down. I immediately jumped back as the poplar rolled off the cherry tree and toward me. I turned off my chain saw and took a close look at the cherry tree. It was bent to the east a couple feet, and had some root damage. But I concluded it would live. Then I noticed, about eye level, a robin's nest, tilted toward me and almost out of the crotch of the tree. It contained two blue eggs. I tilted it back to horizontal and wondered, "Did the mother robin survive the tornado?"

An hour later, I was sitting on my cooler eating lunch, beneath two small trees, the only shade left in the yard. The chain saws were shut down and it was quiet. I heard a robin and turned to see it land on the house roof. She walked down the roof, then flew over to the cherry tree, looked at the nest, and flew away. Deep within,

I smiled: Mother Robin had survived the tornado.

I knew big trucks and end loaders would be coming to remove all the branches, broken boards, siding, and roof shingles from the roadside. I thought about the people, and knew it would be better the day they woke up and went back to bed without hearing a chain saw or big machinery. I knew Mother Robin would nest again and call to her young. And without the chain saws and big machinery, the people could hear the robin.

"Yes," I thought, "less would be better."

Use the Stick and Wade with Confidence

The use of a wading stick will give you more confidence to wade streams wherever trout are found. And when you fish turbid streams where you can't see the bottom, it is an essential piece of trout fishing equipment.

A fall on slippery rocks last year almost put an end to my trout fishing. And it started me thinking about using a wading stick. However, I was hesitant to use the stick. I thought a wading stick was only for old anglers with stiff knees.

About thirty years ago, I read an article written by an old trout angler. He was in his eighties and had stiff knees; it was hard for him, but he was determined to fish trout one more time. Two friends were waiting for him to finish wading his favorite water. They had insisted he use a wading stick. The gray-haired old man, stooped at the shoulders, walked gingerly, feeling his way around slippery rocks with the stick. Occasionally, when he was steady, he made a cast. Wading the stream, feeling the water press against his boots, smelling the balsam, watching a trout hit his dry fly—those were the important things. And knowing it could be the last time, he savored it like grandpa sitting at the head of his Thanksgiving table. The wading stick had made it possible.

He was a good writer, and I imagined that someday I too would write about trout fishing. And, I thought, when I was old I would need a wading stick to fish my favorite stream a last time. Pride too often will cause us (men in particular) to put off making a good decision. I know now I should have been using the wading stick for decades.

The message of this essay is to tell you that you too can benefit from the use of a wading stick. Age is not a factor. Whether you are eighteen or eighty, the wading stick will give you confidence and allow you to fish further and longer. I believe use of a wading stick will help to increase your trout fishing pleasure and your safety, as well as helping you catch more fish.

Last year in April, Pat Hogan, from Trempealeau County, had taken me to one of his favorite stretches on the Rush River, in Pierce County. I was cautiously making my way across rapids to the next pool when my boot slipped off a rock. As I frantically tried to regain my balance, my right knee hit a rock, and I fell spread-eagled into three feet of cold water. Fortunately, I was wearing a wader belt, and was only wet from the waist up. I limped back to Pat's pickup and soaked up the heat as he drove toward home. My knee was bruised. It slowed down my spring fishing, and caused me to wade with a noticeable limp. Fishing with some pain made me think seriously about a wading stick.

In May of last year, I went with Bill Swenson, the retired biology professor from UW-Superior, to Michigan's Upper Peninsula to fish Ernest Hemingway's favorite stream. We were fishing the Big Two Hearted River. My friend Bill, a young man in his sixties who can swim a mile before breakfast, had brought along his wading stick that he used when fishing the Brule River. Bill suggested we wade across the river to have good access to a corner pool. It looked dangerous to wade the swift river when I couldn't see bottom. I broke a dead stick off a cedar tree and followed Bill. He felt his way along the gravel bottom, moving the stick ahead to test for depth. I followed suit, testing the dark water for depth and solid bottom. I was gaining confidence as we slowly proceeded up and across the wide Two Hearted. On the other side, I stuck my stick in the sandbar to use when we returned. Bill had his homemade stick tied to his wader belt, and it was dragging along behind, out of the way.

You don't need to spend a lot of money for a fancy folding wading stick. You probably have an old broom, mop, or rake with a cedar handle. Cut it off so that it is about waist high. Drill a hole about four inches from one end. Use a small rope (parachute cord works well) about two feet long to put though the hole and to tie to the belt on your waders.

The use of a wading stick will give you more confidence to wade streams wherever trout are found. And when you fish turbid streams where you can't see the bottom, it is an essential piece of trout fishing equipment. My wading stick has helped me not only to wade fast water, but to identify and avoid a spongy, loose clay bottom, where I can easily get stuck. And if you have been reading my essays, you know I fish some wild areas where I frequently see bear tracks on sand bars. Now I occasionally rap my cedar stick against a tree to tell an unsuspecting bear that I'm coming through. Using a wading stick will give you a leg up—it's a confidence-builder.

Walk Softly; Trout Can Feel

The median line is essentially a large nerve that runs just under the skin from gill to tail. The nerves in the median line are ultra-sensitive to vibration. If you walk along the bank, the trout can easily pick up the vibration traveling through the water.

Although trout have ear-like structures in their heads, they don't have value for hearing. It is believed their ears are used for balancing rather than serving an auditory function. If you are near trout in a pond or stream and are out of sight, you can make noise by clapping, shouting, or whistling, and it won't have any impact. However, if you shake the ground near the trout, they are gone in a flash.

Fish have a median line, or lateral line; although different from our ear, it serves about the same purpose. This sensory organ is a thin, hair-like line running down the middle of the fish's side. All fish have a median line. In codfish and snook, it is more noticeable than in trout. However, if you look closely, you can see the line in brown and rainbow trout. It appears as a row of scales slightly raised above the others.

The median line is essentially a large nerve that runs just under the skin from gill to tail. It has numerous small branches that extend through the skin and scales to the surface. Through the median line, trout feel water movement, enabling them to maintain their balance, travel erect, and keep their head into the current.

The nerves in the median line are ultra-sensitive to vibrations. If you walk along the bank, the trout can easily pick up the vibrations traveling through the water. In fact, I read where a trout in calm water can pick up vibrations from an unstable bank, like a bog, at a distance up to one hundred feet. I believe the median line is even more important than the eyes to warn trout of danger.

You know by now that I fish upstream, out of sight of the trout. But out of sight is not out of mind. You make vibrations when you wade upstream or down. However, when you wade upstream, the vibrations don't travel as far—the current washes them downstream. The faster the current, the less distance your vibrations travel upstream. Compare it to the difference between talking into the wind and with the wind.

Vibrations are made in the water by movement of your legs through the water, and by the movement of the gravel and debris you rub together when you step on them.

When I believe I am getting within fifty feet of a trout, I wade very slowly so as not to make waves. Again, the stronger the current I am wading into, the less I will make waves. It's best to wade near shore on the shallow side of the stream. I take a high step as I pick a foot up out of the water. Then I step forward and put the foot back into the water, toe first. With practice, you can do this without making a noticeable wave. By cautiously wading into the current, like a deer, you can come to within four feet of a trout.

August 9, 1975, I was fishing Milancthon Creek, in Richland County, Wisconsin. This is a small stream that flows into the Pine River. It has some deep pools hollowed out below limestone cliffs. Milancthon Creek is one of the most beautiful trout streams in Wisconsin. Even if you don't catch a large trout, just being there is an enjoyable experience. I fished three hours in the morning and landed a high-jumping, scrappy brown trout. It jumped clear of the water twice. The big male battled hard in the clear, cool water below a limestone cliff.

I moved further upstream to the next limestone cliff pool. This one faced north, and provided constant shade—ideal for a large brown trout. I waded slowly upstream and made a cast to the head of the pool. On the retrieve, my spinner was ten feet from the rod tip when I noticed something following. I was standing motionless, only my hand moving the reel handle. The big brown had its nose almost on the spinner. Two feet from the rod tip, it turned and swam back to the head of the pool. I waited a few seconds and then slowly backed out of the pool. It was ten o'clock in the morning—late in the day for a big fish to hit.

At 6:15 a.m. the next day, I was slowly wading upstream at the tail of the pool. It took me fifteen minutes to get into position for my first cast. With each step, I made a little wake, less than one inch—about what a deer would make. Sure, I was anxious. I practically had this fish mounted on my wall. But I talked myself into being calm, slow, and deliberate. Finally, I was at a point where I could make a good cast to the head of the pool.

Three feet into the retrieve, the spinner stopped, and the battle was on. I kept the big female in front of me and she stayed deep. Several times she shook violently, trying to rip out the hook. When she tired, I eased her into shallow water, reached around her gills, and carried her up the bank: a heavy, colorful, five-and-a-half-pound brown trout that has graced my wall for years.

When I look closely at my Milancthon Creek brown trout, I can see the median line and I am reminded to wade slowly, like a deer.

Trout can feel vibrations in the water so you should learn to wade slowly on the shallow side like a deer. The author's son, Dan Thurston, uses this technique to cast for trout in the White River of Bayfield County.

Getting Lost Js a Waste of Fishing Time

After an hour of following his compass, he didn't find the river.
Then, instead of sitting down to think, he frantically concluded his
compass was not working... He walked northwest into the setting
sun and into the Bibon Marsh.

Two years ago, the day after I fished the Flag River, my son Dan called. "How's the trout fishing, Dad?"

"Good, with the exception of yesterday."

"What happened yesterday?"

"I took a shortcut when fishing the East Fork of the Flag."

"Oh no, not one of your famous shortcuts!" Dan exclaimed.

Taking shortcuts to return to the vehicle is what I learned from my dad, Dan's grandfather. But shortcuts don't work in the Lake Superior drainage basin. The streams are geologically young, and the river valleys narrow. If you head to high ground to walk the ridge back, you run into gully after gully. You're going up and down hills, through the trees and brush. It's a waste of fishing time.

Last summer when I fished the East Fork of the Flag, in Bayfield County, I was prepared. Using a geological survey map, the Port Wing Quadrangle, I made a copy of the Flag River and highlighted the area I planned to fish. It was easy to see how one could take a shortcut and make a mistake. The East Fork flows north, then makes a sudden change of direction to flow west and join the West Fork. With my map and compass, I fished with confidence. I was able to fish longer, fish further upstream, and catch more trout because I knew the easiest way back was down the stream.

Can you imagine getting lost in the Bibon Marsh, alone, with darkness approaching? It happened to a friend of mine. Though men can get momentarily turned around, they seldom get lost. It's embarrassing to get lost, so I won't reveal my friend's name. July 1993, he was fishing the Long Branch upstream from a bridge north of Grand View, in Bayfield County. He assumed, as I had on the Flag, that the stream flowed basically in one direction. Wrong. He made a mistake and tried to take a shortcut, exactly where the Long Branch made a big curve and changed direction. After an hour of following his compass, he didn't find the river. Then, instead of sitting down to think, he frantically concluded his compass was not working. I know what he was going through; I have been there, but not in the Bibon. My friend decided to follow the sun—it's always accurate. And he walked northwest into the setting sun and into the Bibon Marsh. It took him two hours to walk three miles through the Bibon between the Long Branch and the White River. It was dark when he came out on Town Line Road. He was exhausted from the ordeal, but relieved when a friendly northlander picked him up and delivered him to his pickup.

I learned four important lessons from my friend's near-tragic experience. First, always have a good compass with you, and never question the compass. Second, if you get turned around or lost, stop for at least ten minutes to think through your options before making a decision. Third, because trout streams can throw you a giant curve, have a map with you of the section of stream you plan to fish.

In the summer of 1976 my dad, Ford Thurston, and I went to Amasa, Michigan, to fish brook trout with Cliff Dahl. I was intrigued with Cliff's artistic ability to tie flies, craft fly rods, and make trout creels. He was far more than an artist casting a fly. My plan was to catch an eighteen-inch brook trout for the wall. Cliff's plan was to put me in position to catch the trout. At 6:00 p.m., Cliff parked his Scout at the end of the logging road and we walked a deer trail to his secret stream. Dad and Cliff would fish downstream. I would fish upstream a mile to a corner pool above a small beaver dam. Cliff knew of a brook trout in that pool measuring a solid eighteen inches. After catching the trout, my instructions were: "Walk west to the ridge. Turn and walk south down the ridge to the big pine. There, at the base of the ridge, you will find a deer trail. Take the deer trail southwest to the Scout. We'll be waiting for you." We were deep in the heart of the Upper Peninsula, in wild country, and Cliff had me repeat his directions.

While fishing upstream to the pool, I encountered a series of small beaver dams. It was enjoyable fishing; I was catching scrappy eight- to ten-inch native brook trout.

The sun had set when I arrived at the pool of the big trout. I approached, wading into the current like a deer, slowly and cautiously, so I wouldn't make waves. The trout went for my lure; there was a big swirl, but I didn't feel a hit. It takes trout up to twenty minutes for their pupils to adjust to gathering darkness. Thus, that big brook trout hit short. I made five more casts and then gave up so I could find the deer trail before dark. Rather than wait for the trout to clearly see my lure and hit solidly, I made the right decision and quit fishing.

It happened almost three decades ago, and Cliff's directions are still crystal clear. Maybe I should go back and fish morning, instead of evening, for a big brook trout in Cliff's secret stream.

Lesson number four: Fish morning; if you get lost, you have all day to find your way out of the wild.

At Ninety-Three He Is Still Fishing Trout

Sure, I caught lots of trout over the years. But whenever I had enough trout for a meal, I quit fishing. Often it was one big trout. I still don't understand why some people take more fish than they can eat in one meal.

– Charles Hansen, Mason, WI

At ninety-three, Charles Hansen of Mason, Wisconsin is still fishing trout. When I visited Charles and his wife Clara in August, he promised to take me trout fishing when the time is right. After fishing trout for almost a century, Charles knows exactly where and when to fish. He showed me pictures of big brown and steelhead trout that he and Clara had caught. They ranged in size from five to ten pounds.

Stream fishing for Charles Hansen began as a five-year-old from Ashland, Wisconsin. In 1914, he learned to stream-fish in Bay City Creek. He was that proud barefoot kid that you only see in pictures today, that kid walking to the creek with a tree branch for a pole, store string for a line, a bent pin for a hook, and worms for bait. Charles caught minnows in the small creek near his home and became hooked on fishing.

By the time Charles was fourteen, his dad was chief operator at the White River Power Plant, south of Ashland, along Highway 112. The family had moved to a home on the north side of the river near the hydroelectric plant. From there it was a two-mile walk to Deer Creek, where Charles refined his stream-fishing skill, and usually returned home with brook trout for the table.

While still a teenager, Charles began working with his dad as a maintenance man. His job was to clear wood from in front of the dam and thaw ice out of the gates in the spring. Preparing the gates for opening in the spring prior to the flood was an important and dangerous job.

While Clara, a good cook and devoted wife, was serving Charles and me a chicken dinner, I heard from the spry ninety-three-year-old about some of his narrow escapes. With a twinkle in his eye, Charlie (as Clara affectionately calls him) told me about some of his near-death experiences. "I have had more lives than the average cat," he said. But that is another story.

Prior to 1933, there were two operators at the dam. Each operator worked a shift of twelve hours. In 1933, the forty-hour workweek became a reality, and three operators worked the White River Dam on eight-hour shifts. Charles Hansen was hired as the new operator. He worked the dam until 1947, when it went automatic and he was reassigned to Superior Falls on the Montreal River. When that hydroelectric facility went automatic, he became operator at the Big Falls plant on the Flambeau River, near Tony, where he stayed until he retired in 1971 at age sixty-two. And through all those years, Charles continued to fish with the same childhood enthusiasm as that barefoot boy fishing Bay City Creek.

While eating a piece of Clara's blackberry pie Charles looked at me and said, "I had real good exercise trout fishing. Sometimes, I would walk all day when I went fishing, hunting, and trapping. People don't walk anymore, like they used to." I was beginning to understand why this ninety-three-year-old gentleman, with a mind as crisp as a frosty autumn morning, could still fish trout.

He continued, "Now I do most of my fishing below the White River Dam when trout come up to spawn. Sure, I caught lots of fish over the years. But whenever I had enough trout for a meal, I quit fishing. Often it was one big trout. I still don't understand why some people take more fish than they can eat in one meal."

I asked him, "Is the White River as good today as it was when you worked there as an operator over fifty years ago?"

"Oh no," he responded. "It's not nearly as good as it once was. There's too much erosion. Sometimes the river is red with clay. I don't know how the fish can breathe in that thick water. Years ago, when the water was clear, you could catch five-pound smallmouth bass below the dam. Something has to be done to improve the river. Maybe the state should buy all the land along the river, plant trees, and fence it off from cattle to protect the stream banks from erosion."

I asked Clara how Charles liked to have his trout prepared. She proudly responded, "I have smoked, baked, broiled, and fried trout for sixty-seven years, since we were married."

Charles countered, "I guess I like them broiled best now. But some of those large trout Clara smokes are sure tasty."

As we walked outside toward my pickup, Charles took me to his woodshed. "You know, I have always liked the warm feeling you get from wood heat. So I cut and split my own wood." It looked to me like he was well on his way to having stored a winter's supply of firewood. On the way to the White River, where Charles was going to show me his favorite fishing spots, I decided I would continue to cut and split my own firewood. And maybe, just maybe, when I am ninety-three, I will still be fishing trout—like Charles.

GREAT CATCH - Charles Hanson with one of the large brown trout he has caught in the White River.

You Build It and They Will Come

The money from the trout stamp fund is available, so if it isn't used elsewhere in the state we'll use it here... Anglers can see what we have done with their money and they are pleased. Besides improving the resource, it's just good public relations.
— Dave Vetrano, DNR, La Crosse, WI

When you improve the habitat for trout, they will come. And soon anglers will discover the excellent fishing, and they too will come. That was certainly part of the story when Pat Hogan and I fished with Dave Vetrano last June.

We were fishing Timber Coulee Creek in Vernon County. Between casts, Dave talked about structures. "The original log wing deflectors were built in the water on the outside bend, and they tended to fill in with silt, primarily due to the anchor log at the head of the structure. The lunker structures we developed and now use are more durable, and they don't silt in."

I flipped my spinner toward a corner and the current carried it under the structure as I began the retrieve. A solid strike, and a scrappy eleven-inch brown went airborne. I released it back into the rich limestone water. Dave said, "These trout have been educated; some have been caught and released five times. We now have anglers coming here from fourteen states. You won't catch another in this hole; let's move up."

We took a break in the Coon Creek watershed where Aldo Leopold had helped to establish the nation's first conservation watershed area in 1934. Gradually, as a result of improved farming practices, water run-off was slowed, and each year less silt washed off the slopes to settle in the valley and damage trout stream habitat. However, cattle continued to roam stream banks, and in-stream cover was lacking.

As a member of the Coulee Region Trout Unlimited Chapter, based in La Crosse, I helped install wing deflectors in the spring of 1978 in Bergen Coulee Creek. With money from the trout stamp fund (passed in 1977) and volunteer help, we improved the cover and spawning habitat for trout in the Coon Creek feeder stream. Early in July of 1978, in less than twenty hours, thunderstorms dumped seven inches of rain in the region. A week after the storm, I walked the banks of Bergen Coulee Creek. I discovered that two thirds of the structures had been washed out in a pastured area, and one third in the non-pastured area. Taking that sad walk down the ravaged banks of the little creek told an important story. Where trees, brush, and grass grew—in a non-pastured area—the current was slowed considerably, and less damage occurred to trout stream cover during the flash flood. So working with the farmer to install fencing, while still allowing cattle to have some access to stream water, is a vital ingredient of trout stream habitat improvement. The North Fork of the Trempealeau River in Jackson County, near Hixton, is a good example of that kind of cooperation.

I asked Dave Vetrano, fishery biologist for La Crosse, Monroe, Vernon, and Crawford Counties, how he managed to improve so many miles of trout stream habitat since his arrival on the scene in 1980. "When you look at this region, you basically see trout streams. I only manage one lake of any significant size, so most of my time and energy can be devoted to improving trout streams. The money from the trout stamp fund is available, so if it isn't being used elsewhere in the state, we'll use it here in the Coulee Region." He continued, "Anglers can see what we have done with their money, and they are pleased. Besides improving the resource, it's just good public relations."

That afternoon in June we fished the Little LaCrosse River, in Monroe County. Dave wanted to check on some habitat his crew had completed in May. Pat nailed a chunky fifteen-inch brown, and then I had a solid hit from a fish that jerked free. "Man, that one looked like a twenty-inch fish!" I exclaimed.

"Notice how the bubbles are coming around the corner and moving right next to that structure where your trout hit," Dave pointed out. "That is exactly how it should work, with the main current moving food into the structure where the trout are holding. I have an excellent crew and don't have to keep checking on their work. They know exactly what to do. And it doesn't take an engineer to know how to place lunker structures in a trout stream. If you fish trout, you know how the current creates holding places for trout. So you look at the stream, read the water, and basically go with the flow. It's not that complicated, to where you have to spend a lot of money on research and surveys. Nature has a tremendous ability to heal itself—we just give it a little help."

Pat Hogan and I wondered how long it takes before trout move into new structures. Dave Vetrano explained, "We completed one structure on the West Fork of the Kickapoo and then stopped for a lunch break. When we finished eating, one volunteer from Trout Unlimited took out his fly rod and caught a thirteen-inch brown from under the structure we had just finished." With a broad grin, the trout stream steward concluded, "You build it and they will come."

Tunnel Vision Can Improve Your Trout Fishing

When it came to fishing, Uncle Orville [Thurston] had tunnel vision. He believed whenever you went fishing, you should concentrate on one species of fish. And you should use one lure—the lure you have the most confidence in.

It's often best to be purposeful with your plan when it comes to trout fishing. Too often, in our anticipation of having good fishing, we tend to over-plan—to plan too much. And as a result, we become distracted from the main event. Last summer, I was trout fishing with my nephew, Lee McDaniel from Cashton, Wisconsin, in a stream that flowed through a golf course. Early in the morning, we not only had excellent trout fishing, but we also found golf balls. While one angler cast into a corner pool, the other searched for and recovered spent golf balls.

We discovered that the stream, where it meandered through the golf course, had been ignored by trout anglers. However, at one point we got too caught up in looking for golf balls and scared a large brown that looked to be twenty-four inches long. It was in a feeding position at the head of a pool, shaded by a large black willow tree. When it scurried back under cover, it stirred up at least a dozen trout from fifteen to twenty inches. That twenty-four inch brown trout could now be twenty-seven inches long. When we return, we will ignore the golf balls and concentrate only on trout fishing.

I learned a lot about trout fishing techniques from my dad, Ford Thurston. However, it was my uncle, Orville Thurston, who taught me the valuable lesson of purposeful planning. When it came to fishing, Uncle Orville had tunnel vision. He believed whenever you went fishing, you should concentrate on one species of fish. And you should use one lure—the lure you have the most confidence in. Uncle Orville believed you would fish harder and longer when you used the lure you had been successful with in the past. When we were in grade school, about sixty years ago, every summer Uncle Orville and Aunt Helen would invite me and my cousin Donald Thurston to spend two weeks with them fishing at a resort in northern Wisconsin. The first week, we fished only northern pike. The second week, after the bass season opened, we fished only bass. And we were very successful.

When fishing for northerns, we used a daredevil lure. I recall one day when we went out early before breakfast and fished about four hours. We came in with eleven fish, all over twenty-four inches. Uncle Orville believed we could catch lots of fish, so there was no need to keep what he called skimpy fish. He established his own size limit.

During the second week, when we fished for bass, we could use only a top-water bait called a Plunker. One day I put on a Crazy Crawler. The bass weren't hitting that morning and Uncle Orville accused me of scaring the fish with my "stupid wild splashing Crazy Crawler." It went back into the tackle box in permanent retirement.

By the third summer of fishing at the same resort, we were becoming rather well known for catching big northern pike and largemouth black bass. I recall one guest coming out and motoring up to our boat. "How are they hitting?" he inquired.

Uncle Orville responded, "Not doing much this morning. We have been throwing plugs for two hours, and only have one decent bass."

"Well, if you experts can't catch them, there is no need in me trying." He started up his outboard and motored back to the cabin without putting a line in the water.

Five years ago, when my nephew Lee McDaniel was sixteen years old, I taught him how to fish trout. And I kept it simple. We waded up Fish Creek (in Bayfield County) and cast a number two Mepps red-and-white spinner. We caught and released some nice-sized brown and rainbow trout that June morning. The next year when Lee came to visit, I showed him how to tie trout flies. Now he can decide: fly rod or spinning tackle. Lee has been taught well by his dad, Wayne McDaniel. He plans with purpose, keeps it simple, and always seems to catch fish.

Of course, there are exceptions. Twelve years ago, in early April, after stopping in Winter to visit my dad, Diana and I drove to Iron River with the intent of fishing steelhead on the Brule. However, the snow was melting fast, causing the river to rise and the water temperature to drop—poor conditions for trout fishing. Fortunately, we had an alternate plan, and had brought along our ice fishing gear. We went to Delta Lake that warm afternoon in early April and caught a limit of bluegills and crappies. Dad was pleased when Diana prepared a feast of panfish fillets that evening.

So yes, you should have a plan—you should be purposeful. However, sometimes it helps to have a Plan B in case Plan A turns out to be a bust. Just try to keep each plan uncomplicated—like my late Uncle Orville always did.

Lee McDaniel and the author fished trout next to a golf course. They caught trout and recovered spent golf balls. Failing to concentrate on trout they chased a 24 inch brown out of feeding position to cover.

Survival of the Coaster Brook Trout Is No Easy Task

Saving this beautiful fish is time-consuming and complex. It will not happen without improving the stream environment and without catch and release.

Wild brook trout, more than any other fish to swim fresh water, forecast the health of the environment. Native Americans, trappers, explorers, and early settlers drank of the water where brook trout swam. Even I, without hesitation, drank of that pure water when I worked for the forest service in the mountains of Montana forty-five years ago. But when man entered the watershed to cut down evergreens, mine for minerals, plow steep slopes, smother grass with concrete, and pasture the floodplain of trout streams, it all changed. The brook trout was the first fish to tell us those changes were not good for Mother Earth. Finally, after more than a century of degradation, we are beginning to hear the message from the forest and the stream.

Why has it taken over one hundred years to hear the message? Because it is a message of silence that only the mind can hear. The forest didn't whisper from the quaking poplar to warn us of rapid water runoff when all the evergreens were cut. The stream didn't call from the rapids and say, "My spawning beds are ruined. Flooding has torn out my cover that protected trout from predators. Where I was once narrow and deep, I'm now broad and shallow." And anglers that failed to hear with their minds kept wading the Fish, Whittlesey, Sioux, Cranberry, Flag, and Brule to fill creel after creel with the speckled trout with their delicious, orange-colored flesh.

With an environment that could only produce fewer fish, and man's continued desire to eat them, what chance did the coaster brook trout have?

We know the coaster is to the brook trout what the steelhead is to the rainbow. The coaster spends most of its life in Lake Superior. And like the steelhead, it returns to the streams to spawn. Chequamegon Bay was teeming with large coaster brook trout in the eighteen hundreds. Three- to four-pound coasters were easy to catch over rock and gravel and near river mouths. Today it's a challenge to find any survivors. If only the coaster were a distinct species of fish, then it could be listed as endangered—which technically it is. However, as yet, scientists have not found that it is genetically different from the brook trout.

The potential loss of this colorful fish from Lake Superior and the streams flowing into it has the attention of anglers, citizens, and public officials. Survival of the coaster is in question. We know we need to improve the environment for the coaster. Let's not waste time arguing over where to start.

A first step on the ladder of success is to educate anglers who fish Chequamegon Bay, so they can tell the difference between the coaster and the splake. A second step is to inform anglers of the need to release all brook trout they catch from cold, free-flowing streams entering Lake Superior. A third step is to encourage and pass regulations to protect the coaster. Wild Rivers Chapter of Trout Unlimited, located in northwestern Wisconsin, is actively involved in all the above steps.

Efforts to restore the coaster brook trout by the Wisconsin DNR and the U.S. Fish and Wildlife Service are labeled experimental. There is no guarantee of success. An experiment, proposed for Whittlesey Creek and Bark River (in Bayfield County), is aimed at improving the reproductive habitat and recommending catch and release only for brook trout on those two streams. A second experiment is for Lake Superior waters (regulated by the State of Wisconsin) to have a twenty-inch minimum size limit on brook trout and a one fish per day bag limit.

Wild Rivers Chapter of Trout Unlimited has a picture of a twenty-inch brook trout (no doubt a coaster) that was shocked in Chequamegon Bay, near the mouth of Whittlesey Creek, in the fall of 2001. Somehow, despite our past indifference, the coaster has managed to survive in a few select places. Saving this beautiful fish is time-consuming and complex. It will not happen without improving the stream environment and without catch and release.

We must be patient. Saving the coaster from extinction will not happen in a couple years, or even a few decades. I'm reminded of the king who wanted to plant a black walnut tree. A knowledgeable advisor questioned the king and said, "Your Highness, it will take a lifetime to grow a walnut tree." The king responded, "Then we don't have a moment to waste. We must plant the tree now."

Let's hope future generations don't continue to ask, "Where have the coasters gone?"

Where Have the Coasters Gone?

Has anybody seen where coasters have gone?
They fed lots of people and then passed on.
The child casts and casts without a bite
All coasters but a dream in the night.
Gone from gravel where they had begun,
The clear water now dirty in its run.

A Secondary Stream Should Be Part of Fishing Plan

We are fortunate, in most of Wisconsin, to have many trout streams in close proximity. I prefer the secondary stream to have some natural reproduction and to be a drive of thirty minutes or less from my primary stream.

When you plan a trout fishing venture, it's a good idea to have two streams in mind. Instead of planning to fish just one stream, you should also have a secondary stream. Many times, for me, it has been the secondary stream that has provided the big trout of the day, the trip, or the season.

After I fish the primary stream for an hour without any action, I leave for a secondary stream. Someone may be fishing ahead of you on the primary stream and scaring all the trout. Instead of driving around the back roads looking for a place to fish, or worse yet, going home, you have another choice—your secondary stream. Usually the secondary stream is close, often within ten miles of the first choice.

You may be fishing a section of water that doesn't contain trout. In the winter, trout often move downstream to deep water holes; in the spring they move to seek food, and in the summer they swim upstream to cooler water. We can easily figure out, within an hour, that we haven't found where the fish are holding. Sometimes it's a simple move further upstream to cooler water. Often, though, it's a drive of a few miles to the next stream—the secondary stream.

We are fortunate, in most of Wisconsin, to have many trout streams in close proximity to choose from. I prefer the secondary stream to have some natural reproduction and to be a drive of thirty minutes or less from my primary stream. Streams with natural reproduction have good-quality water and are generally more productive. Use the guide titled *Wisconsin Trout Streams* (also called "The Blue Book"), published by the Wisconsin Department of Natural Resources, to help you find good secondary streams. The book number is PUB-FH-806-2002, and it's available at a Wisconsin DNR Service Center. You can find a listing of service centers by going to the website, www.dnr.state.wi.us.

On a camping trip in August 1984, I planned on fishing Rush River in Pierce County. When I wasn't able to catch a brown over fifteen inches in the Rush, I went to my secondary stream, Lost Creek. It's a small, cold-water feeder stream that flows into the Rush River. Wading upstream in the evening, I caught and released two nine-inch brown trout the first hour—from 5:30 to 6:30 p.m. Then, as the setting sun put the small stream in a shadow, I came to a deep pool with log cover. My first cast allowed the spinner to make the magic turn near the log. The spinner stopped, I set the hook, and thought for a brief second I was into the log. Then my line started to move downstream under the log into the pool below. Fortunately my six-pound test line held as I turned the big trout into the current and up from under the log to the head of the pool. There the battle continued until I was able, after the third attempt, to land the heavy brown trout. She measured just short of twenty-five inches, and I estimated her weight at about six pounds. In the cold water of Lost Creek, it was a successful release. I watched her swim back under her log cover, where she probably stayed and became a gift to another angler.

The Rush River, one of the best trout streams in the state, is heavily fished. At that time (in the 1980s), small Lost Creek with its natural reproduction was largely ignored and was an excellent secondary stream. Thus, it's a good idea to choose as your secondary stream water that has largely been ignored.

When fishing Bayfield County and on the Flag River, I have two secondary streams, the East and West Fork of the Flag. When I'm not having any success on Fish Creek, and I'm parked on Fish Creek Road, I can fish up my secondary stream, Pine Creek, without moving my pickup. When trout are not responding on the Sioux River, I fish upstream on one of the most beautiful streams in Wisconsin, the Little Sioux River.

Remember, when you go trout fishing have two streams in mind. It can give you an opportunity to enjoy exploring new water, discover a "secret stream," and maybe catch the largest fish of the season.

Teaching an Old Friend to Spin Fish

He had a tendency to wade up the middle of the stream. I showed him how to stay in the shallow water and cast across into the deeper water.

It had been twenty years since we had seen each other. And forty-eight years since we had fished trout together. There he was, standing broad-shouldered at my door the morning of June 12, 2001. We looked into each other's eyes and shook hands. Then two men in their sixties embraced. An embrace that said it has been so very long.

Ronald Abegglen and I had been corresponding by e-mail for six months. Then he informed me he would be near Hayward, Wisconsin, on a fishing vacation. I encouraged him to come up for a visit and some trout fishing. I introduced him to my wife and dog. We sat down at the kitchen table to talk family, fishing, and old friends.

Ron claimed I taught him how to fish fifty-two years ago. We called ourselves "Garden Hackle Purists." Using only worms, we fished downstream. Exactly as Dad, Ford Thurston, had taught me, I taught my friends. We lived about twenty-five miles northeast of Madison in the small town of Fall River. By the time I left for the army on a Greyhound bus in 1953, Ron and I had fished every trout stream in Columbia County. We talked about our last fishing experience, a week before I boarded that bus, when we limited out on brook trout.

Ron brought along a new pair of waders and a spinning rod. He wanted to learn how to wade upstream and spin fish for trout. Ron had logged over half a century of fishing downstream with worms. Now he wanted to learn a new technique. It would be a tough task for the student and the teacher.

We fished above the Pike River Road on the White River, in Bayfield County. Despite lots of rain, the White still flowed clear, and we found plenty of small hungry trout. Exactly what was needed for the novice spin fisherman.

I showed Ron how to cast by holding the rod, above the reel in one hand, releasing the bail, and holding the line firm in the other hand. Then, with movement at the wrist to flex the rod, make an underhand cast by releasing the line. At first he was doing too much of a sidewinder swing, causing the spinner to fly too far right or left. Then he was moving his arm too much at the elbow with very little wrist action, causing the lure to arch too high and get caught on tree branches. He said, "I should have tried this at home in the yard."

"You're right," I responded, "but here you are, being force-fed knowledge on the fast track."

Wading upstream was giving Ron some trouble. He had a tendency to wade up the middle of the stream. I showed him how to stay in the shallow water and cast across into the deeper water. "The spinner works better," I explained, "when you retrieve in a cross current rather than downstream. And it's the action of the spinner that attracts trout to hit." Then, to emphasize my point, I made a cast across the river where the water cut under a cedar tree and a log. A scrappy fourteen-inch brown hit, jumped high, and then bore down under the log. I brought it back and kept it fighting into the swift current. It soon tired. Ron took a picture and I released the White River brown.

After an hour of casting, Ron was doing well. My friend had been an excellent high school athlete, and I could see talent in his casts. He was holding his casting arm close to his side and flexing at the wrist instead of the elbow. The cast was flatter, and Ron was able to sail his spinner under overhanging tree limbs. His accuracy was causing me to be an enthusiastic teacher. "Great cast!" I exclaimed.

Early the next morning we were parked along my secret trout stream. It was raining. We were talking and eating venison pepperoni. This was not down time; it was good time: we had lots of catching up to do. Ron told me of how the old streams we had fished were now being loved to death—too many homes had been built along their banks. He said his favorite stream was the Trempealeau River, in Jackson County. I told him that when I had lived near La Crosse, I had often fished the Trempealeau and it was a favorite of mine. We looked at each other, knowing we may have been on the steam at the same time in the 1970s and 80s. Then Ron said, "All the years I fished the Trempealeau, there was one guy I often saw early in the morning who fished upstream."

"Where was that on the Trempealeau?" I asked.

"Between Davis and Lincoln Road," he responded.

"Ron, that is where I always fished the Trempealeau! I would walk down the tracks and fish it back upstream to the road."

Ron looked at me, smiled, and said, "I fished downstream and walked back up the tracks."

While waiting for the rain to let up so we could fish my favorite stream, I asked, "How come you never said anything to me?"

"You had a mustache at the time; I didn't recognize you! Besides, you don't talk to other fishermen on your favorite stream. Isn't that what you taught me?"

The author teaches an old friend, Ronald Abegglen, a new technique to cast the lure under overhanging tree limbs.

Longtime Nemesis: That Darn Net

The mistake many anglers make when playing a large trout in a river is to stay put, not move, and let the fish run downstream. It's best to get in the river, downstream from the fish...and force the trout to work upstream into the current.

Sometimes when you are trout fishing, you can't get along without a landing net. However, I find it almost impossible to have a good relationship with a net. They easily get hung up and are downright unfriendly.

Dad told me about nets that seek revenge for being stretched out when caught on brush. The stretch cord stretches to a max and then lets go. If the darn net hits you between the shoulder blades with full force, it can drop you to your knees in pain. Maybe because it happened to Dad, I have been especially careful to avoid a solid blow from my net. When I'm cutting corners on a trout stream and feel the pull from my net that is caught on a dead balsam branch, I stop to free it. Apparently, the angler who left a net hanging from a tree this summer along the Cranberry River didn't stop to release it. Maybe he or she thought the net would release on its own. No way—you release it, it punches you in the back, the cord breaks, or it separates from the handle.

After a while, you tire of releasing the net from the branches. The landing net causes you to lose valuable fishing time, so you leave it at home. And then, as luck would have it, you hook a fish too big to handle without a net.

Until seven years ago, I had not carried a net for decades of trout fishing, and I had successfully landed trout up to twenty-six inches. June 19, 1994, when on Fish Creek in Bayfield County, a twenty-seven-inch steelhead smashed my spinner. I immediately moved to the tail of the pool and stood in shallow water to play the fish into the current. The mistake many anglers make when playing a large trout in a river is to stay put, not move, and let the fish run downstream. Then you are contending with the weight and power of the fish and also the force of the current. It's best to get in the river, downstream from the fish in shallow water, and force the trout to work upstream into the current. The force of the current is against the fish and it will soon tire. Three times, I reached around the gill plate of that twenty-seven-inch steelhead with my hand. But my fingers were too short. This was a heavy fish, and I couldn't get a solid grip on it. I even tried to grab it around the tail. But due to the protective slime on the steelhead, I couldn't hold it. My third option was to slide it up on a sand bar then grab it, turn it upside down, and carry it up the bank away from the water. That worked, and I was able to remove the hook, measure it, take a picture, and then release the big steelhead. Why turn the fish upside down? It disorients the trout and it will usually hold still while you remove the hook.

The day after landing the twenty-seven-inch steelhead, I was shopping for a landing net. I immediately discovered that most nets were too small for large trout. Trout net makers have it all wrong. The average-sized hand will land trout under twenty-four inches. For those fish, you don't need a net. Yet all the trout nets seem to be designed for trout under twenty-four inches. Sure, they are beautiful, with wooden handles crafted from cherry, walnut, and maple. They are called catch-and-release nets. And they are shallow—only eight to fifteen inches in net depth. Don't take that beautiful and expensive net trout fishing; put it on the wall for decoration. A large trout can spring right out of it.

You don't have to believe the angler with the tiny net who tells you it's important to net the trout so you can release it quickly. That same angler is probably using a light action rod, has a small pound test line, and has to play the trout until it's exhausted before bringing it to net. Then the net is so small that big trout can repeatedly jump out. Obviously, some of those big trout when released are too stressed to survive.

The net I finally settled on for steelhead and large brown trout, has a depth of twenty-seven inches. However, a heavy twenty-eight-inch steelhead from the Cranberry River taught me a lesson in April 2000. It curled up in my net and then jumped out to continue the fight for freedom. When I brought it back a second time, I turned the net to close it and prevent the fish from jumping out.

Now, whenever I think I may catch a large fish over twenty-four inches, I carry my net. However, I do take some precautions to prevent it from getting hung up. I hold it with my rod and point it through the brush. The cord from the handle is stretched over the frame, so the netting isn't flopping around trying to catch a branch. Also, when I am walking through the woods, I put a plastic bag over the net and wrap a rubber band around the plastic bag at the handle. Remember, I always wade the stream, so the trailing net seldom comes in contact with branches as I fish upstream.

If I don't forget this net on some remote section of stream, it should last for years. The last net I had, over forty years ago, I left along the stream after landing a large trout. Two days later, I went back to retrieve it only to find the webbing had been chewed by mice. That net is still hanging in my workshop. I would have repaired it long ago, but it's too tiny for any self-respecting northlander steelhead.

Stream Programming Is Good and Bad

Being programmed simplifies life. But it doesn't make it more
challenging. Therefore, it's both good and bad. I suppose we seek a
balance between simplification and challenge in our daily living. It
seems to me we should also seek that balance in our trout fishing.

Katie, our black lab, is programmed for a walk twice a day. It's OK if we take the same walk each day. She seems to prefer that.

The chipmunks came out of hibernation in late March. Twice last summer, when I tapped on one particular tree with my walking stick, a chipmunk appeared. Twice out of two hundred times—one percent—was enough to program Katie: she was programmed to stop at the hollow tree stump on our daily walk.

So she climbed up the snow bank to the hollow tree on March 31, raised her ears, and looked at me as only a lab can. "Hit the tree, 'Old Guy!'" Katie ordered. I tapped on the hollow tree with my walking stick. Katie looked up eight feet to the top of the stump, expecting a chipmunk to appear. Guess what—the next day, and the next, the same program. "This could go on all summer. This dog is programmed," I told my wife, Diana.

At eight thirty one Thursday morning, I was at a restaurant in Iron River. The waitress brought me a cup of coffee and asked, "The usual?"

"Yes," I responded. No need to make a decision; I'm programmed. I eat breakfast out every Thursday. Been doing it for years.

Being programmed simplifies life. But it doesn't make it more challenging. Therefore, it's both good and bad. I suppose we seek a balance between simplification and challenge in our daily living. It seems to me we should also seek that balance in our trout fishing.

If you continue to fish the same trout stream, you will certainly learn it well. However, you are missing the challenge to explore and find new beauty in nature.

A trout fisherman told me that in one year he caught and kept over two hundred legal trout from a two-mile section of his local trout stream. He literally ruined the reproductive resource of that small stream in one season. The following year it was difficult for anyone to catch more than one legal trout, on that stream, on any given day. Yes, if you are programmed to fish the same stream day after day, and you don't practice catch and release, you can literally ruin the fishing in your favorite stream.

In 1996, I made a list of thirty trout streams to fish within seventy-five miles of my home near Iron River, Wisconsin. I never fish the same water twice during the season, unless I'm returning to try for a large trout that I saw. Last year I was on Fish Creek four times and never fished the same water twice. I fished a total of eight-and-a-half hours and released twelve trout. I figure, unless someone else caught and kept those trout, most of them should be there. They will be larger this year, and more fun to catch. I am programmed to release trout, and that is good for both you and me.

I haven't fished all thirty streams on my list. Some, when I fish them, I cross off because they have poor habitat for trout. Usually, each year I find out about a stream I can add to my list. We are fortunate, here in northwest Wisconsin, with hundreds of miles of quality water for trout. I have 319 miles of trout stream I could fish in the thirty streams. Although I usually fish trout twice a week, I still manage to cover only about sixty miles of trout water during a season. With all that water to explore for large trout, how can I become programmed when it comes to trout fishing?

One of the streams on my list is the "Wild West"—my secret trout stream. I sometimes see a boot print along the "Wild West." But I have never seen an angler fishing it. Most people probably fish it once, don't have any success, and never return. Because they fished the lower half, and didn't catch any trout, they assumed the whole stream was poor.

Maybe it's best if you are not programmed to explore trout streams. If you continue to explore, you will end up on the upper half of the "Wild West." And, if you can get away from work, the best time for you to be there would be Thursday morning. That's when I'm programmed for breakfast at a restaurant in Iron River.

Grocery Store Confusing,
Trout Stream Familiar

On the trout stream, when you come to deep water with logs, you take time to study, to read the water, for exactly where a large trout will be hiding. The only time you stop the cart in the grocery store is when a lady with two kids is blocking your way, or your wife is looking for a coupon.

Have you noticed that grocery stores get bigger each decade, while during your lifetime trout streams have remained relatively the same size? And the larger the grocery store, the more confusing it becomes. Granted, a large trout stream is more difficult to read than a small one, but it isn't confusing.

In early August I stopped at a bank in Iron River, Wisconsin. "How are you, Jay?" Sandy asked with a smile.

"Real well; I went out for breakfast and had time to think about the grocery store and the trout stream. Sandy, I really feel comfortable on the trout stream, but put me in a Super Center and I am confused. It takes too long to find stuff."

"Oh, I don't like large grocery stores either!" Sandy exclaimed as she cashed my check.

Sally was passing by and heard the conversation. "Super Center grocery stores are all supposed to be designed the same way with the same layout."

"Right," I responded. "They are all designed the same way: to confuse men."

On the way home, I started thinking about the conversation at the bank. I have lived long enough to remember how friendly, familiar, and warm grocery stores used to be. They were a lot like the small-town bank still is today. If you couldn't find something in the small grocery store, you knew someone to ask.

My wife is a skilled navigator in any grocery store. The bigger it is, the better she seems to like it. When I'm going to town to purchase something for the outdoors, she will give me a short grocery list. And I will go to the smallest grocery store in town. The item might cost a little more, but at least I can find it and come home feeling successful.

The last time we went trout fishing, Diana was following me—just like I usually follow her in the grocery store. I pointed out a small opening between two branches at the head of the pool. She made a perfect cast and nailed a fat brown trout, fifteen inches long. I was proud of her excellent presentation.

The last time we were in a super-large grocery store, Diana was shopping for the home and also helping me. I had a list of items to buy for the annual Isle Royale fishing trip. As usual, I was pushing the cart when she sent me off to find my blue cheese salad dressing. After five minutes of wandering, I started reading the signs high above the aisles—exactly where no one looks. Finally, in the correct aisle I spotted a thirty-foot long shelf of salad dressing. It took five more minutes to find the bottle with a white substance that looked like blue cheese. After another five minutes of searching, I found Diana. She had a box of crackers and was looking through her coupons. "Here it is," she said. "I can save on two boxes, and crackers are on your Isle Royale list."

"Yes, to go with the soup and salad," I responded as I placed the bottle in the cart.

She looked at the bottle of salad dressing. "But I thought you wanted blue cheese instead of ranch."

She didn't send me off on another search. I white-knuckled that cart handle. In the next aisle, I saw a man who had stopped his cart to look at the cans of Bush's Baked Beans. Maybe he had a golden retriever and was dreaming about grouse hunting. He jerked to attention when his wife called from the end of the canned food aisle, "Come on, Harold! Quit gawking! I have a lot of shopping to do."

On the trout stream, when you come to deep water with logs, you take time to study, to read the water, for exactly where a large trout will be hiding. Then you decide on the approach so you can present your lure without scaring the fish. The only time you stop the cart in the grocery store is when a lady with two kids is blocking your way, or your wife is looking for a coupon. When your wife keeps moving, it just adds to your confusion.

After my trip to the bank, I told Diana about my conversation with Sandy and Sally. Then I stated, "You never seem to be confused in a grocery store, even a large one you go to for the first time.

And I'm always comfortable on a trout stream—even one I'm fishing for the first time. After fishing streams of all sizes, I just know where the trout will be hiding. Why is it you're always comfortable in a new grocery store?"

"Remember when we started dating, I was working in a grocery store?"

"But that was a small store."

Diana ended the conversation with, "All grocery stores, large and small, have a certain flow to them."

Guess I haven't waded through enough grocery stores to identify the flow. That's why I push the cart, like all the other men you see tagging along behind their wives.

If You're a Trout, It's One Meal a Day

The ultimate truism of fish is this: the colder the water, the slower their body utilizes food; therefore, the less food they need. And the warmer the water, the faster food is absorbed; therefore, the greater their need for food.

When a lot of food is present in the stream, a trout can get enough to eat for the day in less than two hours. You could do that too, if you had the stomach for it. But most of us are accustomed to eating three times a day. And most of the year, a trout can't get by with only one meal a day either, because there is just not enough food available in their stream.

Trout streams change, and in the heat of summer, most become a warehouse of food. It is then, in July through August, that trout have a smorgasbord of food available. They can feed to capacity in less than two hours. Knowing that trout will go on a feeding binge at a particular time each day during July and August is probably the most important information I can give an angler. But first, some background information.

Because the metabolism of trout speeds up as the water temperature warms, they have a need for more food in July and August than any other time of the year. Neat, isn't it, that they need more food exactly when more food is available? Mother Nature keeps surprising us with the adaptability of its wild species. Bear have an abundance of food to eat in summer and early fall, just like trout. And, like trout, they put on weight to carry them through winter, when very little food is available. And the metabolism of bear, like that of fish, slows down to compensate for the lack of food. Bear, though, have been given a unique advantage over trout. They sleep for the five coldest months of the year, and their energy needs slow down to a trickle.

The ultimate truism of fish is this: the colder the water, the slower their body utilizes food; therefore, the less food they need. And the warmer the water, the faster food is absorbed; therefore, the greater their need for food.

I found one study that reported trout over thirteen inches will digest a two- to three-inch minnow in only twenty-four hours when the water temperature rises above sixty degrees. And during July and August, in most of our trout streams, the water temperature during the day will rise above sixty degrees.

Both terrestrial and aquatic insects are abundant during summer and early fall. Grasshoppers, crickets, and ants are plentiful. And in the warmer water, aquatic insects frequently hatch out. Then, too, frogs, crayfish, and minnows are usually more abundant in summer. So trout are practically living in a fast-food restaurant. They can get all the food they need, when they want it. That is the key to good summer trout fishing—when they want it. With food all around them, when will they decide to eat?

The trout of summer usually decide to eat their one big meal early in the morning. And I believe there are three reasons for the early-morning feed. First, the temperature has cooled down during the night, and the water temperature is comfortable for them early. Trout, like us, like to eat when they are comfortable.

Second, trout seek shade. And brown trout, the trout most frequently available in our streams, seek shade eighty-four percent of the time—more than brook and rainbow trout. So to be successful, you need to fish early or late, when the stream is in shadow. However, with the abundance of food available, the trout of summer can get enough in the morning to completely eliminate the evening feeding time.

Third, large trout over fifteen inches have learned that their number-one predator, man, is seldom around at 6:00 a.m., so it's a safe time to feed.

In those streams that are heavily fished, the early-morning time—the time you should be on the water—will begin in June. On June 9, I parked near the Big Rock Campground and walked upstream on the well-worn path along the Sioux River, in Bayfield County. I knew exactly where I was going that morning before the first rays of sun hit the water. It was the big pool less than half a mile above the campground—probably the best hole on the river.

Near the middle of the pool, I had a solid strike and was battling with an energetic, high-flying spring-run steelhead. After releasing the twenty-four-inch fish, I moved to the head of the pool. My next cast brought up a larger steelhead, about twenty-six inches. This one, I thought, had been caught previously. She jerked back and forth—no fast surges or high jumping. All her energy went into trying to jerk out the spinner. Then she rolled, jerked again, and was free. I smiled when my line went limp, and bid farewell to a smart fish.

It all happened between 6:30 and 6:45 a.m. in a large pool with easy access that is heavily fished. Good trout fishing, during the summer, requires that you rise early to be on the stream when trout eat their big meal.

Good trout fishing during July and August requires that you rise early to be on the stream when trout eat their one big meal.

Gamefish Are Too Valuable To Be Caught Only Once

Trout live in a hostile environment where they must survive drought, flood, ice, predators, and muddy water. Those who say most trout that are released don't survive simply don't understand trout. This is no namby-pamby fish. It is a stouthearted survivor.

It was in 1939, when anglers were trying to fill their creel and their stringer, that noted angler and conservationist Lee Wulff (1905-1991) made the legendary statement, "Gamefish are too valuable to be caught only once." Wulff was a trout fisherman who invented the fishing vest and could tie trout flies without a vise. He produced nine award-winning TV films, wrote eight books and hundreds of articles, and took time away from the trout steam to teach about the ethics of fishing. I don't know of a human being who gave more to both the angler and trout than Lee Wulff.

In April, I was on Fish Creek three times, and met four anglers. Only one was wearing a trout creel. I believe about twenty-five percent of trout anglers fish with a trout creel and don't practice catch and release. Over sixty years ago, the only anglers on a trout stream without a creel were those who couldn't afford to purchase one. So, in my opinion, trout anglers have come a long way since 1939 regarding catch and release. In this essay, my intent is more to inform you about what is new regarding catch and release than to convince you to change your habits. I believe if you are better informed, you will be more likely to practice catch and release. But I am an eternal optimist, one who believes every dog can hunt and the largest trout of the day is just around the next corner.

The next time you cross a rapid trout stream, stop and look at the rushing water. Visualize how high the water was during the spring flood. Then contemplate how trout live in a hostile environment, where they must survive drought, flood, ice, predators, and muddy water. Those who claim that the majority of released trout don't survive simply don't understand trout. This is not a namby-pamby fish; it's a stouthearted survivor.

I have kept records since 1976 of every trout I have caught over nine inches long. And each year I enter in my trout logbook over one hundred trout. So we're talking here of approximately three thousand trout from nine to twenty-eight inches long that I have caught and released since 1976. By 1985, I was getting fairly good at releasing trout, and I estimated that ninety-five percent of the trout I released survived. Since 1990, I have used a new release technique and pushed the survival rate to ninety-eight percent. That is correct: ninety-eight trout out of every hundred that I catch now survive. Of course, I'm not a bait fisherman. Research evidence all across the country has shown a higher mortality rate for fish caught and released by those who use bait. Research has also shown no difference between fly and spin fisherman. And the jury is still out on whether you can achieve more success with barbless hooks. Hooks with barbs don't penetrate as far, and the depth of hook penetration can kill fish. However, you can save time when releasing a fish caught on a barbless hook, and time saved getting the fish back in the water promotes survival.

How many times can you catch and release the same fish? Studies done on Timber Coulee Creek, in Vernon County, by noted trout researcher Dr. Robert Hunt, indicated the average brown trout was caught and released five times, and the average brook trout fifteen times. Also, I read a recent study that found the more a trout is caught and released, the less stress placed upon the fish—they seem to become acclimated to catch and release.

OK, what are some of those techniques I use which can help you increase your trout survival rate? First, upgrade to a longer pole with stiffer action and a stronger pound test line. It takes longer to play a fish with light action equipment, and that can result in a lower survival rate. I now use a medium-light action (instead of light or ultra light), seven-foot spinning rod with eight-pound test Fireline (instead of four- or six-pound test). I can bring fish to net faster, and as a result have been able to present my lure to more trout while increasing the survival rate.

The second important survival technique is to immediately turn the fish upside as soon as you land it. When stomach up, the trout is disoriented, and holds still while you remove the hook and measure the fish.

The third technique, and the one that really boosted my survival rate from ninety-five to ninety-eight percent, is to remove the hook, spinner, or fly from a fish hooked in the gills backward, from under the gill cover. Most fish hooked in the gills do not survive if you try to remove the hook through the mouth. It's just about impossible to do this without damage to the gills. And damage to the gills will usually kill the fish. Cut the line with a needle-nose pliers. Then, while holding the trout upside down, lift the gill cover up and reach in with the pliers. Gently extract the hook out backward under the gill cover. This technique works on trout ten inches or larger.

You don't have to wait for Christmas or a birthday to give a gift. It was Lee Wulff who also said, "The fish you release today is your gift to another angler."

Bridge Fishing Js Good For Summer Trout Fishing

It works best on a cloudy day after a rain. You fish the bridge hole and the first hole above and below the bridge. Then you drive to the next stream and continue.
—Clarence "Simon" Schultz, Washburn, WI

In June, a high school friend would be coming to Bayfield County to fish trout with me. And I knew stream fishing for him could be a problem. I told my wife, "Ron had trouble wading Fish Creek and the White River last year. I don't know where I can take him trout fishing." Like some other senior citizens, Ron has knee problems, and he can't wade pain-free for more than a couple hundred yards. Diana suggested canoe fishing. But I ruled that out because the good areas for stream fishing would require a portage.

Three days before Ron's arrival, Diana and I were on our way to Darlington (in southwestern Wisconsin) for a canoe race. We came to a detour, and I got out our *Wisconsin Gazetteer*. I directed Diana to take County K through the valley of the Big Green River. When we crossed the river, at Werley, I told Diana about a brown trout caught under the bridge that weighed twelve pounds. And the idea hit home. I would take my friend bridge fishing.

Clarence "Simon" Schultz, renowned trout angler from Washburn, told me about his tactic of bridge fishing. He said, "Jay, it works best on a cloudy day after a rain. You fish the bridge hole and the first hole above and below the bridge. Then you drive to the next stream and continue until you catch a limit of trout. Years ago, I would start fishing at Whittlesey Creek, and before I got past the Lost Creeks, by Cornucopia, I would have my limit." I thought it strange I had never read about bridge fishing as a trout fishing technique. Maybe it was just too obvious.

The evening in June when Ron arrived, it was raining and the forecast for the following day was cloudy weather. Conditions were looking good for Simon Schultz bridge fishing.

Our plan was to drive north from Iron River, Wisconsin, and see if we could get as far as the Cranberry River. Our first stop was a bridge on the Iron River. We discovered both of us could fish the hole under the bridge. One angler could cast under the bridge from the upstream side, and the other cast upstream from below the bridge. And it worked. We fished beneath six bridges and caught trout from under four of them.

Most serious trout anglers assume the bridge hole is heavily fished. Although that may be the case around the general opener in early May, during the summer months you seldom see anglers fishing from bridges. As Simon Schultz indicated, after a rain, trout move around. And they frequently move back and forth from the first good hole above the bridge to the first good hole below the bridge. If there is a good hole under the bridge, a large trout may take up residence there after the fishing pressure has diminished. Big trout prefer holes where there is constant shade. So remember when you go trout fishing, if you start at a bridge, always make your first cast under the bridge.

Ron and I took turns fishing up- and downstream. We varied the time from fifteen to forty-five minutes before meeting back at the bridge. And we discovered it never took more than twenty minutes to find and fish that first good hole. When we took forty-five minutes at a bridge, we both ended up fishing beyond the first good hole. Surprisingly, the second or third hole never seemed to be as good as the first one above and below the bridge. It reinforces the theory that a number of trout are moving under the bridge and close to the bridge. And for us, it was a waste of time to fish further away from the bridge. It slowed down the technique, and we ended up bridge fishing fewer streams.

In four hours, Ron and I fished six bridges. The clouds evaporated by 11:00 a.m. and we stopped fishing.

Bridge fishing was better than we had anticipated. At each stop, we caught fish. Ron lost a big fish above a bridge on the Iron River. He yelled, and I came running with the camera. But the big brown, about twenty inches, was off before I was in position for a picture. Ron caught a colorful brown trout of thirteen inches in the first hole below the bridge on small Schacte Creek. And I had a large brown, about seventeen inches, hit in the first hole above a bridge on the Flag River.

We caught and released brook, brown, and rainbow trout. It proved to be a learning experience for me, and a safe, memorable experience for my friend.

If you bridge fish by yourself, it will take longer, so plan to spend about forty-five minutes at every bridge. Will I do it again? Absolutely; it's a great early-morning trout fishing technique to use in the summer. You catch trout with very little physical exertion. Then you relax in air-conditioned comfort on the way to the next bridge.

Prime Time: When Yellow Leaves Are Falling

During September, when the water is cooling down, you will have excellent fishing morning and evening. If you want to sleep in, no problem; fish late, and you will still have the stream to yourself.

One of the reasons we fish trout is to find solitude. Therefore, we should spend more time fishing when others do not leave tracks along the trout stream. Having a stream to yourself is "prime time."

Trout fishing is heaviest during May and June. It decreases considerably after July Fourth. On some streams, fishing is nonexistent during the last two weeks of August and the month of September—with the exception of Labor Day weekend.

In addition to finding solitude, you are also likely to find your best fishing during the last six weeks of the season. My goal is to convince you that late season—August 15 to September 30—is "prime time." If you consider the following, you may decide to increase your trout fishing after August 15.

Phototropism begins about August 15. And it's nature's first signal of fall. The days are shorter, the nights cooler, and the water temperature begins to drop. It's a message for fish to move and feed. You will feel a hint of fall in the air that raises your energy level, and you will notice the first leaves decorated in red and yellow.

Trout are larger in September. A September trout is about three inches longer, and considerably heavier, than it was when the regular season opened in May. The September fish makes a better picture and is more fun to catch and release.

Both morning and evening fishing are productive in September. During the warm days of June, July, and most of August, your best fishing is early in the morning. During September, when the water is cooling down, you will have excellent fishing morning and evening. If you want to sleep in, no problem; fish late, and you will still have the stream to yourself.

Rainfall during late season will put fish in a feeding frenzy. We usually have less rainfall during the last six weeks of the season. Therefore, rainfall at this time will change the pattern and provide food for hungry fish. My dad, Ford Thurston (an excellent musky fisherman), fished August and September, after a slow gentle rain. On those special fish feeding days, he always caught a legal musky. During late summer, you too should fish the slow gentle rain days. Trout, musky, walleye, and crappies respond—and you often have no fishing competition.

If you know where a large trout hides, watch your rain gauge and fish for the lunker after approximately a half-inch rainfall. That old trout knows food is being washed into the stream. With some turbidity for cover, the big trout will move to the head of the pool to feed. You know where the trout will be holding, and success is practically guaranteed.

Trout become more predictable in September, and are easier to find. Most of our trout streams contain brown trout. The brown, a native of Europe, has been extensively fished for centuries and, as a result, has become smarter than brook and rainbow. Brook and brown spawn in the fall. During phototropism, as the water cools, spawning trout begin their upstream migration. In the waning days of summer, brook and brown trout become more aggressive. Their upstream travel utilizes energy, and they are hungry fish. It's easier to outsmart a brown trout during the last six weeks of the season.

There are fewer mosquitoes to distract you. Trout fishing is more enjoyable during the mosquito-free cool days of late summer. Recently, I was fishing the South Fork of the White River (Bayfield County) with Steve Amann, from La Crosse. He was armed with mosquito repellent and was amazed he didn't have to use it. Steve explained he had fished near La Crosse in late August and had been attacked by swarms of mosquitoes. I smiled and said, "It's more comfortable to fish in September, Steve!"

In late September, as yellow leaves are falling, fish the pools near the gravel beds, in the upper one-third of your favorite stream. You will have solitude, you will appreciate nature's artwork, and you will catch heavy, brightly colored trout. It's "prime time!" Need we ask for more?

157

— JAY THURSTON —

Potato River, the Prettiest Trout Stream

Man is a part of nature and only as a part of nature does he really matter.
— Frank Lloyd Wright, Architect

Many people might find it hard to believe an angler would consider a river named Potato to be the prettiest trout stream in Wisconsin. But on October 10, during peak color, I would have argued with anyone about my conviction concerning the Potato River.

As we slowly worked our way up and out of the steep valley where the day, the river, and two people came together to enjoy rare natural beauty, my friend Pat Hogan said, "It's too bad this river is named Potato. The name doesn't do anything for its beauty."

Pat had driven north from his home in Trempealeau County to go trout fishing. Together we had waded many good trout streams all over the state, but this one named Potato was unique. When Pat arrived at my house I told him about the Potato River below the lower falls, near Gurney in Iron County, where it was open for trout fishing. I mentioned the difficulty of walking down into the valley and then back out. I told Pat, "We'll pace ourselves and enjoy the scenery on the way in and out."

I put two bottles of Gatorade in the back pocket of my trout vest and we headed downhill on a crystal-clear morning. We were slowly descending the steps when we came to a landing and looked southeast for our first glimpse of the waterfall. A bright sun was easing into the valley and glimmering on the water tumbling down the fall. Streamers of silver splashed on dark bedrock to land in a deep pool at the base. We took our time to enjoy the scenery and saw more than water where trout might swim.

We cast spinners into a corner pocket beneath a steep ledge—great holding water. To our right we could see and hear the waterfall. Our reels turned and so did our eyes, up the water-carved walls to the yellow poplar leaves shimmering in the breeze. When you're with a good friend in a special place, it doesn't matter if you catch trout. It's trout that got you there, and you're fortunate to live in an area where wild trout swim.

Pat looked at me, stopped reeling, and said, "Jay, thank you for taking me here. Neither of us knows how much time we have left. But if I could choose, I would go with a smile on my face remembering this place."

When we turned to move to the next pool, Pat saw two pop cans and a plastic bottle. "Look, Jay, someone doesn't get it! They don't understand. Why did they come here?" I picked up the litter and placed it in the back pocket of Pat's trout vest.

Beneath the silver waterfall at the big pool carved out by ten thousand years of plunging water, two trout anglers cast artificial lures for trout. I moved left near the falling water. Pat moved right near the deepest part of the pool. For a while, I was alone in my own world, then I wondered where Pat had gone. I turned and saw him sitting down, relaxing. I walked back and sat down next to Pat. We forgot about catching trout. That special place on the Potato River took center stage. We looked up. The wind blew, and leaves were set free. We watched yellow leaves, shining in the bright sun beneath a deep blue sky, waltz back and forth in the breeze. They floated down to the river. Some landed in the pool beneath the waterfall.

Close to the sound and strength of plunging water in the steep-walled valley, we had become a part of nature. I recalled the words of Frank Lloyd Wright, the architect who used the natural environment in his designs: "Man is a part of nature and only as a part of nature does he really matter." Pat asked about the Native Americans and if they had come here to fish hundreds of years ago. We thought they probably had, because the waterfall provided a natural barrier where fish would gather in the fall. But we couldn't be sure, since they had left the valley as they found it. "Pat," I said, "this area remained natural and undisturbed until people with cans and bottles showed up." Then, near the center of the pool, we saw an otter staring at us—maybe wondering what we were talking about. It nervously went down, then came up to stand taller in the water. We sat still and quiet. It came closer, and was joined by a mate. Gradually they settled down and started to fish. One came up on the far side of the pool with a sucker about twelve inches long. It ate part of the catch and then moved on to share with its mate.

We left the fishing to the otter and slowly worked our way back up the trail. Two anglers, who took time to let their minds float free, like yellow leaves gently swinging in a breeze, knew in their hearts they had been to the prettiest trout stream in Wisconsin.

POTATO RIVER BEAUTY - Beneath the silver waterfall in a pool carved out by ten thousand years of plunging water Pat Hogan, from Trempealeau County, cast an artificial lure for trout.

Can You Keep A Secret?

One unwritten rule lies in being taken to fish a new lake or stretch of river. Such confidences are a secret trust between friends, and it is a betrayal of that trust to show such places to another angler.
                              – Ernest Schwievert, *Trout* magazine

Can you keep a secret? Secret trout stream, that is. Three years ago, when I started writing these trout fishing essays as newspaper articles, I mentioned that I had a secret trout stream. I wrote, "I will share most of my secrets. One, the name of my secret trout stream, I plan to keep for a while—in the end, though, if you read the columns, you'll know." At the time, I thought I would run out of material and that would be the end. Then I would stop writing about trout fishing—essentially, I would have nothing more to say. Life is not like that, is it? We continue to learn, to question, to wonder, to be amazed, and to try and put a handle on new and interesting events. That is precisely why as long as our spirit flows, heart beats, and brain functions, life is worth living—and trout fishing, for me, is worth writing about.

Since this began over three years ago, I have had a lot of compliments and only three complaints—all having to do with a secret stream. One angler said, "Jay, you really hurt me when you wrote about the South Fork of the White River." It was a favorite stream of his, a secret. Another angler I met on Fish Creek said, "It's OK for you to write about all those other streams, but not this one." Fish Creek was obviously his secret stream. An articulate angler sent a long e-mail concerning an article I had written about the Cranberry River. He was concerned that hordes of "outsiders" would come, like they had come to the Brule, and the trout resource in the Cranberry River, his favorite stream, would be destroyed. My response: "You expressed a concern about informing the 'outsiders.' I can assure you it won't be the 'outsiders' who destroy the trout resource in your favorite stream. They don't have the time it would take. They don't know exactly where or when to fish your stream. What you and I need to be concerned about is the good fisherman (good in the sense that he knows how to catch trout) who lives near the stream and continues to fish the same stream. He doesn't have the ethics you have to release trout. He doesn't violate, but he keeps all the legal trout he catches. He catches more than he will eat and gives trout to his friends and neighbors. It is not the 'outsider'; it is the 'insider' who will ruin your favorite stream. I saw it happen on two streams in 1975. In one season, a hundred large trout were taken from those two streams, by the same fisherman, and the resource was literally ruined for years. I know—I was that fisherman."

Although I will give you the name of my secret stream, I will not tell you specifically where to fish that river. One of my objectives in writing is to encourage you to expand your trout fishing to participate in the joy of exploration and thrill of discovery. That is why I keep writing about different streams. Eventually, if you fish a lot of streams like I do, you will not have the need for a secret stream. What you will have is a lot of secret places on many streams.

Some of you have shared a secret stream, or secret place, with another, only to find that person couldn't keep a secret. And, without your permission, your secret was shared with others—that is not only disappointing, it is unethical. In an article titled "Angling Etiquette," printed in *Trout* (the magazine of Trout Unlimited), Ernest Schwievert wrote: "One unwritten rule lies in being taken to fish a new lake or stretch of river. Such confidences are a secret trust between friends, and it is a betrayal of that trust to show such places to another angler. Some old-timers valued such trust so highly that they refused to fish such places alone, returning only with the friends who took them there."

As long as I keep writing about trout fishing and confessing where I caught the big fish, I will reveal someone's secret stream. Therefore, it is only fair that I also reveal my secret stream.

I found this river by accident. In 1997, I stopped at a bridge and saw a nice hole, so I gave it a try and immediately caught an eleven-inch brown. The next year I fished the Marengo River eight times, in eight different places, and caught and released fifty-four trout, from nine to seventeen inches. To find the best places on my river, you will have to do a lot exploring—a lot of wading. Most of the Marengo I rate as poor—it is too flat (wide), and filled in with sand. It lacks wood and deep holes for cover. And, like many streams, it goes in cycles. This year is a down cycle. So if you fish the Marengo and have a poor experience, don't give up on it—the river will return, and you should too. Fish it again in a couple years. Keep trying a new area on the Marengo, and eventually you will be rewarded.

You Can Find Gold When Trout Fishing

In the gin-clear water I saw a rock about the size and shape of a potato. It was sparkling—a gold color. With my right foot, I moved it into shallow water and picked it up. Indeed, it appeared to contain gold. . . And finding gold wasn't unexpected. You see, I have found a lot of gold along trout streams.

For years, I have been picking up rocks along trout streams. I have found some nice agates and attractive quartz, but never gold. At least I *had* never found gold—until July 24, 2003. Trout fishing wasn't very good, so I started looking at rocks. And I found a rock that I believe contains gold. (No, I won't give the stream. I don't want a gold rush on a good trout stream.)

It all began at 7:07 a.m. I was casting a silver spinner in the gin-clear water at the tail of a big pool. While standing in water a foot deep, I saw a brown trout, about eighteen inches long, swim toward me. Then it turned and stopped three feet in front of my waders. Before I had time to think of a reason for the trout's strange behavior, the dark head of an animal popped out of the water eight feet to my right. An otter was looking directly at me. And just as quickly as it had appeared, it was gone, swimming frantically upstream beneath the tag alders. The brown trout waited a few seconds and then swam slowly upstream beneath the tag alders. One of the most unusual events I have seen on a trout stream happened in less than ten seconds.

It was not a good day for me to fish trout—at least not if I expected to catch a lot of fish. The stream was too clear and the sun too bright. But I was there to get some exercise and to enjoy being part of nature.

I waited a couple minutes, and then proceeded to wade upstream. My steps were slow and deliberate so as not to make waves. I was being cautious in case that unpredictable brown trout should surprise me a second time. However, nothing happened, because the otter, a better fisher than I, had frightened all the trout.

Then I began to wonder about that otter, because two strange things troubled me. First, he was fishing downstream. Second, he was after the largest and smartest trout in the pool. But he was a small otter—probably a teenager, big-eyed and short on experience. Most otters, from what I had observed, always fished upstream. An otter will sneak up on a trout by approaching from behind, in its blind spot. Essentially, they fish upstream like I do. Junior's decision to go after a large, smart brown trout was indicative of his inexperience. But most amazing was the behavior of the big brown trout. He was fleeing from the otter when he saw me, turned, and stopped. He seemed to be using me for protection from the pursuing otter. A trout using logic—is that possible?

After fishing for an hour, a large hornets' nest caught my attention. It was five feet above the water and constructed in the crotch of an alder. I moved in close and snapped a picture. Some disturbed hornets immediately circled my head. They were objecting to the flash in their eyes at three feet. I backed off and took a wide circle around the nest.

Continuing to fish the small stream, I managed to catch and release two nine-inch rainbow trout. It's a pretty stream, shaded by timber with a lot of fine gravel, rapids, pools, and some interesting rock bars.

Just past the hornets' nest, I was slowly working through some rapids with my wading stick. The sun was coming in over my left shoulder and I was looking down. In the gin-clear water I saw a rock, about the size and shape of a large potato. It was sparkling—a gold color. With my right foot, I moved it into shallow water and picked it up. Indeed, it appeared to contain gold. And not just on one side. Particles were shining all around the rock. I don't pretend to be a geologist. I'm someone who has always been interested in rocks and has collected a few good samples from trout streams. If the trout aren't hitting, I look at other things, including rocks. And this day I hit pay dirt.

As I write, I am looking at my rock. It is sparkling, and I know those small deposits in the granite and quartz rock could be mica. A scratch test would probably tell me. However, the glittering particles also look like they could be iron pyrite—fool's gold. Maybe an acid test would tell me. Or I could take my rock to an expert for analysis. But I don't have to do any of those things, because I really did find gold. And finding gold wasn't unexpected. You see, I have found a lot of "gold" along trout streams. As I have said before, there is a lot more to fishing than catching trout. I'll keep my golden rock to remind me of the otter and the large brown trout, the hornets that objected to the flash of my camera, and the golden memories yet to come.

Moving Because the Trout Are Calling

Within ten miles of that house (in Viroqua, Wisconsin) are ten trout streams. And within seventy-five miles of Viroqua, an avid angler can fish most of the top streams in Wisconsin and some of the best trout water found in the United States. Yes, the trout are calling.

Why would a person move when they are happy—when they really like where they live? For me, it's the trout. As my wife says, "The trout are calling."

I have fished enough trout streams around the state of Wisconsin to know where the best streams are located. And it's to that location, in southwest Wisconsin, where the trout are calling me. Fortunately, I am married to a lady who understands that when the trout call, her husband listens.

So we have sold our residence here in the northland and purchased a house in Viroqua. Viroqua is a city of about 4,300 people in Vernon County—thirty-five miles southeast of La Crosse. Within ten miles of that house, I have ten trout streams. That is about as good as it gets in Wisconsin. And within seventy-five miles of Viroqua, an avid angler can fish most of the top trout streams in Wisconsin, and some of the best trout water found in the United States. Yes, the trout are calling.

To move from our lake where the North Fork of the White River begins, in Bayfield County, to the hills and farm country of southwest Wisconsin was not an easy decision. Moving to northern Wisconsin and living on a lake was the fulfillment of a dream. My wife and I agonized over this move for more than a year. It's not easy to leave a place you really like—a place where you feel comfortable and you call home. I have enjoyed writing about the northland. And through my writing, I have met a lot of good people. It's hard to leave when kind people keep telling you they like what you write. But the trout are calling.

Claire Duquette, the editor of *The (Ashland) Daily Press,* gave me my start as a freelance writer of trout stories and then as an outdoor writer in general. I'll forever be grateful. Not knowing how many years I have left to write, or how long I can still do a good job,

I have decided to concentrate on what I do best—write trout fishing stories. When I taught school and worked with children on creative writing, I always told them to write about what they know best. So I guess I'm practicing what I preach.

Since we are moving, I'm not sure where the writing road will lead. But I plan to return and fish my favorite streams that flow into Lake Superior. The trout will call me back, particularly in the month of May, because that is when I have caught and released a lot of steelhead from twenty to twenty-eight inches. And I'll send Claire Duquette a trout story from time to time.

There were a few years after I retired from education in 1995, and before writing trout stories, that I gave motivational speeches to school kids and teachers. Whenever I talked to high school kids, I always asked them where they lived. They seemed confused by the question and were often hesitant to venture an answer on something that seemed so obvious. None that answered gave the correct response. They frequently gave the name of a city or an address for the answer. "Wrong," I would say. "You live where you are right now. Your body is where your heart is, where your spirit is, where your brain is—that is your home." Then I asked the sixty-four-dollar question: "What are you doing to take care of your home?" And follow-up questions. "Do you buckle up the seat belt every time? If you don't, you can be ejected in an accident and destroy or cripple your home. Your home could end up in a casket or a wheelchair. Some of you who smoke cigarettes are slowly destroying your home. What can you do to take care of your home, to keep it in good repair? And if you don't take care of yourself, where will you live?" It certainly got the high school kids to think about taking better care of their body—their home.

I live in my body. That is my philosophy. Therefore, it's probably less difficult for me to move than it is for a lot of people—I understand that. By moving to Viroqua, I will have more trout streams to explore and fish. Therefore, I will fish trout more often. And every time I fish trout, I wade upstream against the current, getting great exercise. Trout fishing is good for me—for my home.

The trout are calling—I must go.

Where He Wanted To Go

Slowly he waded upstream
And cast the quiet pool.
Then to the murmuring riffle
And up to the gentle bend.
In the early morning fog
He disappeared from view.
He was gone, he was gone,
Where he wanted to go.

Pinnacle of Trout Fishing:
Jay's 110 Tips Detailed in This Book

1. When fishing for steelhead, it's best to have more than one river in mind.

2. With a good hatch and nothing rising, move on—the trout have.

3. In early spring, trout are in big holes and they need a wake-up call.

4. The joy isn't just in catching fish; it's in experimenting and trying something new.

5. In April, after the snow is gone, big trout are easy to find.

6. Everyone who fishes trout in Wisconsin should have the Wisconsin Gazetteer.

7. In spring when you find one large trout, others are often in the same area.

8. Ask permission; large trout hide where it's posted—areas seldom fished.

9. It's essential to wade in the river in order to keep a low profile.

10. Big trout are usually found under cover at the head of the pool.

11. To get in position to catch large trout, replace hip boots with chest-high waders.

12. The more the stream meanders, the more holes on the outside turn for trout.

13. Fishing is best when you can see your lure at eighteen to thirty-six inches of water.

14. If you can see your lure at a depth of more than thirty-six inches of water, trout are easily frightened.

15. Books often lack clear detail of insects for tying exact imitations.

16. When it comes to catching trout, the kingfisher, great blue heron, and otter are best.

17. The shadow cast by your lure—like that of a kingfisher—will scare trout.

18. Wade upstream on the shallow side, like the great blue heron.

19. Fish upstream in the blind spot of the trout, like the otter.

20. *Large trout are suspicious of a lure that moves unnaturally upstream into the current.*

21. *Check the knot strength of your line every twenty minutes.*

22. *It's the diameter of your line, not the pound test, that trout see.*

23. *Breathable waders make it easier to walk to areas seldom fished.*

24. *You don't do well if you allow an angler to take you out of your normal fishing rhythm.*

25. *In spring, trout feed best when the stream temperature is rising.*

26. *The best weather days for you, when the sun shines bright, are poor fishing days.*

27. *Big trout only come out to feed under the cover of clouds, darkness, or stream turbidity.*

28. *If you want to catch a large trout, wait for the rain and the clouds.*

29. *Trout survive to grow large by being reclusive and hiding in the shadows.*

30. *Release trout: it's a gift to another angler and an investment in the resource.*

31. *When you fish alone, always inform someone where you are going.*

32. *It's not the style or color of clothes that scares trout, it's your movement.*

33. *Wear a wide-brimmed hat and prescription (if needed) polarized sunglasses.*

34. *Mosquitoes are attracted to dark colors, particularly dark blue.*

35. *Make a list of items you need for fishing and keep it in your "trout vehicle."*

36. *Alternating meanders is one way, among many, to fish with a trout buddy.*

37. *Color is important, because trout see in living color, similar to humans.*

38. *If not sure of the color to use, try yellow—all fish are attracted to yellow.*

39. *Experiment to find the color that works best on your favorite stream.*

40. *Bright-colored lures work well in the cold, turbid waters of early spring.*

41. *To wade a swift stream, face into the current and bend slightly at the knees.*

42. *Deliver the lure so it will turn under cover in front of the trout.*

43. *Don't overlook bumpy water; it's good cover for large trout.*

44. *It usually works best to keep it simple, and fish with the lure you have confidence in.*

45. *Big brown trout are known to move up small streams in August.*

46. *If you want to catch big trout, concentrate on streams that produce the most food.*

47. *Hard-water streams, from limestone bedrock, are more fertile than freestone streams.*

48. *Trout hit a lure because they are hungry, it makes them mad, or the lure attracts them.*

49. *Attractors work well, because often when you're fishing, trout aren't feeding.*

50. *A bright-colored lure with chartreuse or pink works well in turbid water after a rain.*

51. *Trout usually feed every day, and in the summer it's often early in the morning.*

52. *Trout are very sensitive to temperature change—even one degree makes a difference.*

53. *Know the water temperature; the fifty-degree rise is a long-held secret.*

54. *The first fundamental for catching trout is to fish where and when others don't fish.*

55. *It is usually safer to wade in the stream than it is to walk the bank.*

56. *Always take a shower and check for ticks after trout fishing.*

57. *Getting lost is a waste of fishing time. Never fish wild country without a compass.*

58. *The more we fish, the more we change—it has been researched and documented.*

59. *To catch trout, your two most important items could be a rain gauge and rain suit.*

60. *Whenever there is a half-inch rain at night, fish early the following morning.*

61. *Under a light misty-type rain, trout are likely to hit all day.*

62. *Each stream is unique, and that is a quality that makes exploring streams exciting.*

63. *You will usually find the best pools with cover in the middle third of the stream.*

64. *Often the lower third of the stream is wide and flat, lacking depth and cover.*

65. *It's OK to keep trout from streams with a high population and a limited food supply.*

66. *Trout taste great when rolled in cornmeal and fried crisp in olive oil.*

67. *The largest trout are often found where there is continuous shade.*

68. *Good holding spots are under the roots of a tree or below a north-facing cliff pool.*

69. *Brown trout like to hide in deep pools with logs for cover.*

70. *A trout doesn't have an eyelid and can't dilate the pupil—it must seek shade.*

71. *A trout has more rods than cones—rods are needed for vision in low light conditions.*

72. *Trout stay deep, near the bottom, to protect the blind spot below them.*

73. *All fish must face into the current in order to maintain their position.*

74. *You can get close to trout when fishing upstream and moving in their blind spot.*

75. *Concentrate on the ten percent of trout-holding water, because ninety percent of the water doesn't hold trout.*

76. *Remote areas are often neglected, and that is where you often have your best fishing.*

77. *For the warmest time of year—summer—fish early during the coolest time of day*

78. *In summer, start early, before sunrise, and you will have three hours of good fishing.*

79. *Fish a wild area early, and you have the rest of the day to find your way out.*

80. *When you retire, you can fish anytime, so don't fish weekends when others are out there.*

81. *Everyone can benefit from the use of a wading stick. Age is not a factor.*

82. *You can make a wading stick from an old broom or rake with a cedar handle.*

83. *Trout have a lateral line of nerves near the skin to identify even slight vibrations.*

84. *Trout are able to feel an angler walk along an unstable bank one hundred feet away.*

85. *Trout can feel vibrations you make when wading downstream toward them.*

86. *Wade upstream like a deer to prevent waves that make vibrations and scare trout.*

87. *When you fish trout with artificial lures rather than bait, you get more exercise.*

88. *Good fishing is often found where lunker structures have been installed.*

89. *It doesn't take an engineer to install lunker structures in trout streams.*

90. *Keep your fishing plan simple—often you don't do well when planning too much.*

91. *To save the coaster brook trout the in-stream habitat must be improved.*

92. *After fishing for an hour and not catching a trout, leave to fish your secondary stream.*

93. *Spin fish with the underhand flip cast when fishing brushy, small streams.*

94. *You should be in the stream to play a large fish and keep it fighting into the current.*

95. *For catch and release, don't use ultra-light tackle.*

96. *The longer you play a fish, the more stress it creates and the lower the survival rate.*

97. *The more streams you fish, the greater your chance to find a real large trout.*

98. *When you come to a deep pool, stop and look for where a large trout might hide.*

99. *The metabolism of trout speeds up as the water warms, and then they need more food.*

100. *Trout eat more in the summer than any other time of the year.*

101. *About the time that most quit fishing—July and August—you can have your best fishing.*

102. *If you use the best release techniques, you can increase the survival rate to ninety-eight percent.*

103. *Turn a trout upside down when removing the hook. It will become disoriented and hold still.*

104. *If the trout is hooked in the gills, cut the line and remove the hook backward from under the gill cover.*

105. *Bridge fishing is a good technique to use on a cloudy summer morning after a rain.*

106. *After phototropism, in August, you can have success fishing both morning and evening.*

107. *Stop, sit down, enjoy the scenery, and listen to the sounds of nature.*

108. *Trout get you there, and it could be the prettiest place you have ever been.*

109. *Eventually you understand you're there not to take, but to enjoy.*

110. *Carry a camera—fill your trout basket with dayflowers and place it on a shelf.*

To order additional copies of

Following in the Footsteps of Ernest Hemingway

or other Savage Press books

call:
715-394-9513
National Voice and FAX orders
1-800-732-3867
E-mail:
mail@savpress.com

Purchase copies on-line at:
www.savpress.com
Visa/MC/Discover/American Express/
ECheck/Accepted via PayPal

All Savage Press books are available at all chain and independent bookstores nationwide. Just ask them to special order if the title is not in stock.

Box 115, Superior, WI 54880 (715) 394-9513